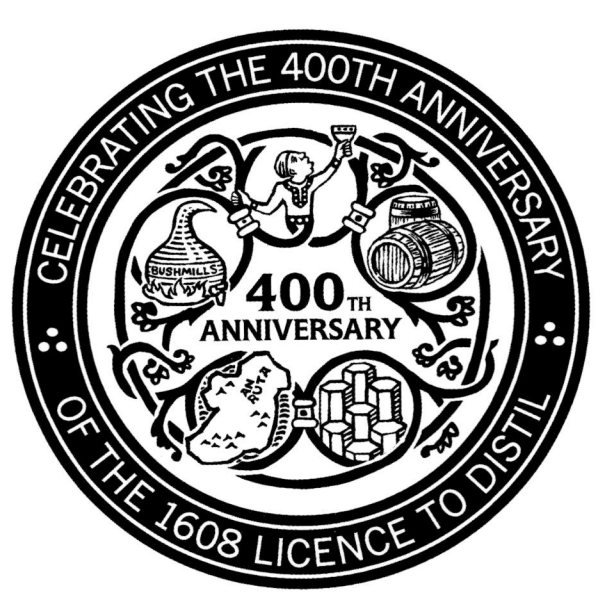

BUSHMILLS

400 YEARS IN THE MAKING

First published in hardback in 2008 by
Appletree Press Ltd
The Old Potato Station
14 Howard Street South
Belfast BT7 1AP

Tel: +44 (028) 90 24 30 74
Fax: +44 (028) 90 24 67 56
Email: reception@appletree.ie
Web: www.appletree.ie

This edition published in 2009

Copyright © Appletree Press, 2008 and 2009
Text © Peter Mulryan, 2008 and 2009
Photographs © as acknowledged on page 186

All rights reserved. Printed in China. No part of this publication may be reproduced or transmitted in any form or by any means, electronic, photocopying, recording or in any information and retrieval system, without prior permission in writing from the publisher.

A catalogue record for this book is available from the British Library.

Bushmills – 400 Years in the Making

Hardback Trade Edition ISBN-13: 978 1 84758 068 9
Hardback Corporate Edition ISBN-13: 978 1 84758 092 4
Paperback Edition ISBN: 978 1 84758 148 8

Desk & Marketing Editor: Jean Brown
Copy-editing: Jim Black
Designer: Stuart Wilkinson
Production Manager: Paul McAvoy

9 8 7 6 5 4 3 2

AP3448

BUSHMILLS

400 YEARS IN THE MAKING

Peter Mulryan

Appletree Press

Contents

Foreword		8	Chapter 17	The Noble Experiment	71
Chapter 1	The Land of Legends	11	Chapter 18	Ireland's Best	75
Chapter 2	Laudabiliter	15	Chapter 19	The Brothers Boyd	83
Chapter 3	The Plague Spirit	17	Chapter 20	Coleraine	93
Chapter 4	Tudor Law	19	Chapter 21	Of Bushmills and Barley	97
Chapter 5	The Plantations of Ulster	22	Chapter 22	Big Business	103
Chapter 6	Modern Times	25	Chapter 23	New York	109
Chapter 7	The Poteen Years	27	Chapter 24	Charrington	111
Chapter 8	Mr McKibben	29	Chapter 25	Irish Distillers Group	117
Chapter 9	'Irish Coffey'	31	Chapter 26	Le Whiskey	127
Chapter 10	What is Whisky?	35	Chapter 27	New Frontier	135
Chapter 11	Small is Beautiful	37	Chapter 28	Memories	141
Chapter 12	Phoenix	43	Chapter 29	The Drink	155
Chapter 13	Single Malt	46	Chapter 30	How to Make Whiskey	161
Chapter 14	SS *Bushmills*	49	The Bushmills Family		178
Chapter 15	20th Century Blues	53	Acknowledgements		186
Chapter 16	Partition	67	Index		187

Left: Approaching Bushmills

Foreword

Bushmills is a small village on the north coast of Ireland synonymous with the art of distilling whiskey. It is a community of people who are proud of their heritage. Centuries of craftsmanship and a willingness to innovate ensure that they look to the future with confidence. They know what it takes to be the best.

Since I arrived here in January 2006 to take over the running of the distillery, I have learned that the people of Bushmills are a storehouse of knowledge about the ancient tradition of whiskey-making.

Such knowledge, hard gained, is not given away lightly. Sit down with the people, pay them respect, share a taste of the local spirit and perhaps they will reveal some of the secrets that make Bushmills famous.

As this book so vividly portrays, creating the smoothness that is the hallmark of Bushmills whiskey is a blend of science and art. The origins of both go back into the mists of time. While this publication marks 400 years of the first official record of whiskey-making in the area, we know

Left: Gordon Donoghue

that the skills of distilling in this part of Ireland have a much longer history.

The area was once dotted with small distilleries; today there is only one. Bushmills is Ireland's oldest working distillery and our whiskey is different from other Irish whiskeys. Here, under one roof, we make and bottle triple-distilled malt whiskey – and it's this unique distillation process that provides the underlying smoothness that characterises our whiskeys.

To make Bushmills requires special ingredients, not least water. Ireland has it in abundance and here on our doorstep the River Bush provides our source. But Bushmills is more than purely physical ingredients. The magic component is time – time for the whiskey to mature in the cask, time for the angels to receive their share. Ageing can't be hurried, so in this part of the world patience is more than a virtue, it's a way of life.

Walking in the footsteps of generations of distillers here at Bushmills is both an honour and a joy for me and I will take great pleasure, when the time comes, in passing on the secrets of our whiskey to those who follow me.

Our great past is brought to life in these pages. The author, Peter Mulryan, captures in detail the business acumen, the people and the skills that have kept this distillery prospering. It's a colourful history of both good times and bad, of a determination to succeed and of the characters that have made Bushmills known throughout the world.

My advice is to savour the story with a glass in your hand. It will help you appreciate that Bushmills is the best Irish whiskey not just because it is the oldest – it's actually the oldest because it's the best.

Gordon Donoghue
Bushmills Distillery

Chapter One

The Land of Legends

If the Giant's Causeway is the 'Ninth Wonder of the World', then the Old Bushmills distillery some two miles south, is surely the Tenth.

The Giant's Causeway, that magnificent place where hexagonal columns form stepping stones that disappear under the sea was created, we are told, by volcanic rock cooling very quickly. But when you are standing there the legend of Fionn Mac Cumhaill (Finn McCool) seems to make more sense. Apart from being a giant and presumably very strong, Fionn is Ireland's greatest hero. According to the legend he built the Causeway so he could walk to Scotland without getting his feet wet.

It is a legend yes, but about 10,000 years ago, around the time of the last Ice Age there was a land bridge between Ireland and Scotland. Maybe people used it to cross from one coast to another. Maybe not, but it is just possible. Around here fact and fiction are curiously interwoven.

There is a small stream nearby called St Columb's Rill and it travels over the same basalt rock that makes up the Causeway, before joining the River Bush and flowing on to the sea. But on the way something quite magical happens – some of the water is transformed into whiskey. It has been going on for some time, some say since 1784 while others say 1608. In truth though it goes back further than that: much further. Whiskey has been made in this area for so long that dates are immaterial; the stuff has woven itself into the fabric of everyday life.

The *Book of Dun Cow* was written in the 11th or 12th century. It is the third-oldest known manuscript in Ireland and it contains another legend. This concerns two warriors who worked up a terrible thirst in battle. So ferocious was this thirst that the rivers of Ireland had to be visited in order to slake it. What is surprising is that alongside Ireland's major rivers, like the Shannon and the Liffey, the story takes time

Left: The Giant's Causeway, 2 miles – or a (giant's) stone's throw – from the distillery.

out to mention the River Bush. Even then, the quality of the water must have been legendary.

There has never been a shortage of water in this part of Ireland, but there is no knowing when the alchemy of distilling arrived. However the magic that turned *uisce* into *uisce beatha*, the 'water of life', can be traced back to the Norman invasion. Yet again legends weave their way into fact, so it is hard to know where one ends and the other begins.

Right: 'One of the King Waters of Ireland' ... a few miles downstream, it turns into one of its finest whiskeys.

Chapter Two

Laudabiliter

In 1155 the Norman King Henry II of England first claimed lordship over Ireland. His claim was based on a Papal Bull issued by Pope Adrian IV. It is often noted by the cynical Irish that Adrian was the only Englishman ever to become Pope.

Henry II needed Papal backing so he could legitimately invade Ireland in order, he claimed, to reform the Church in Ireland. The title of the Papal Bull, or order *Laudabiliter*, means literally 'it is praiseworthy'. The document refers to Henry's intention "to extend the borders of the Church, to teach the truths of the Christian faith to a rude and unlettered people, and to root out the weeds of vice from the field of the Lord..."

The Savages of the Ards is a book about a family called Savage, rather than a book on the wild folk of the area. Published in 1888, it outlines how the Bushmills area fits into the Norman invasion of Ireland.

"With twenty-two Anglo Norman knights and three hundred soldiers De Courcy, encouraged by Henry II, started from Dublin on the venterous invasion in the month of January AD 1177...They pushed their conquest northward 'till they brought, nominally at least, under Anglo-Norman domination a tract of country corresponding roughly to the present counties of Louth, Down, Antrim and half of Londonderry."

The historic land in and around Bushmills lay at the centre of an area controlled by the most powerful of the Norman-Ulster Barons, Sir William Le Savage. His eldest son Robert crops up in relation to *aqua vitae*, in a booklet published by Old Bushmills in 1938: "Away back in 1276 a delightful story is told about Sir Robert Savage, ground landlord of Bushmills and a rare old swashbuckler." It then quotes from the *Annals of the Savages* (sic):

"Sir Robert Savage having prepared an army against the Irish, allowed to every soldier, before he buckled with the enemy, a mighty draft of aqua vitae..."

Left: King Henry II of England

Were it true it would be a great story, but alas it is not. Sir Robert was in all probability dead by 1276 (that or he was a very fit ninety-four-year-old). The story however may relate to his son Henry, who died the following year 1277, but probably it is nothing more than historical Chinese whispers. The tale was in fact lifted and misquoted from a book published in 1812; it should read that every soldier was given "a good dose of good wine or ale".

Let us get the story straight. There is no way of knowing if there was distilling in Ireland prior to the 14th century. It is only then that *aqua vitae* crops up in the medieval Celtic manuscript, *Red Book of Ossory*. This is a work by a Franciscan bishop appointed in 1316, and it contains a recipe for making "aqua vitae" from wine. It is clear then that distilling was not widespread, and was quite probably confined to monasteries. Furthermore when *aqua vitae* is first recorded it does not refer to a spirit made, like modern whiskey from grain, but rather distilled wine. A sort of raw Irish brandy if you like.

If distilling was the preserve of the religious, this might give us an idea as to when it arrived and how it spread across the island. When *aqua vitae* finally arrived, it is more than likely that it left death in its wake.

Chapter Three

The Plague Spirit

The Black Death hit London in September 1348, and by the spring it had laid waste to the country. The Irish Sea was no obstacle – by the following summer, the bubonic plague had taken Ireland.

There was no known cause. Some blamed the wrath of God, but most didn't have time to think about it. Four out of five people infected were dead within a week.

There were numerous talismans and cures, but one of the most promising must have been a liquid born of alchemy: a water that burnt; a liquid so mystical it brought the drinker closer to God; so magical it preserved flesh and so rare it was nothing less than the water of life.

Alcohol, originally prepared by alchemists and later by monks, was commonly applied as a remedy for the Black Death. In the absence of a Health Service, the Church took upon itself the role of healer, and tried to meet the medical needs of its people.

Uisce beatha and the knowledge of how to make it, most probably arrived on these shores with Irish monks, just before or at the time of the great Plague. It is all so long ago, that there are no records or documents, but it is pretty certain that an Arabic culture discovered or possibly even rediscovered the art of distilling sometime in the 11th century. The still or *alembic* was used to strip essential oils from healing plants, to create tinctures. The word *alcohol* is a corruption of the Arabic word *al-kuhl*, which described a very fine powder of antimony used as eye make up (kohl), as well as meaning 'essence'.

The basic technique of distilling is so simple and effective, that little has changed in the way we obtain aromatherapy oils today. Water and the herb to be distilled were placed inside a clay bowl, the alembic was then sealed and a fire lit beneath it. As the water boiled, rising steam stripped the essential oils from the plant. The humid vapours would then pass through an arm jutting from the top, where they would be cooled back to a liquid.

Tracing the evolution of Irish whiskey then is very difficult. For a start there is little in the way of written records and what documents exist rarely make a clear distinction between Roman *aqua vitae* (made from wine), or Irish *aqua vitae* (made from grain). To add to the confusion the Gaelic term *uisce beatha* could refer to either drink, as pointed out in 1600 by Fynes Moryson. In his journal he praised the medicinal value of Irish "*aqua vitae*, vulgarly called usquebaugh."

When the first Irish record of "graine in making of *aqua vitae*" is documented, distilling fever had clearly gripped the land. An Act passed in 1556 by the English Parliament of Elizabeth I in Ireland explains that, "*aqua vitae* a drink nothing profitable to be daily drunken and used is now universally through the realm of Ireland". The legislation went on to make it illegal for anyone, with the exception of course of peers, gentlemen and the freemen of the larger towns to distil *aqua vitae* without a licence from the Lord Deputy.

It was, of course, a law the Irish chose to totally ignore.

In the centuries that followed the Norman invasion, the Hiberno-Norman lords, or the 'old English' as they were known, became in the words of the famous expression 'more Irish than the Irish themselves'. This so worried the Establishment in loyal areas like Dublin, that in 1367 the Statutes of Kilkenny were passed, which attempted to stop those of English descent from speaking Irish or intermarrying. However the Statutes had little effect – life in Ireland went on pretty much as it always had. It is not until the Tudor re-conquest of Ireland that Bushmills finds itself yet again in the middle of an unfolding history, whose ripples can be felt to this day.

Chapter Four

Tudor Law

The Old Bushmills distillery can trace its heritage back to a patent to distil that was granted 20th April 1608. But this being Ireland, nothing is as simple as it first appears. For a start a distillery was not built in 1608, and if *aqua vitae* was made in the area, it was no different from the stuff that was distilled in 1607. The first thing the patent, or licence shows is that whiskey making has been going on in these parts for a very, very long time. The second is that this was the first time the State saw a way of making money out of alcohol.

By the end of the 16th century, England was refocusing its attention on Ireland. The Ulster armies of Hugh O'Neill, along with those of his son-in-law Hugh O'Donnell, were locked in battle with the troops of Queen Elizabeth I of England, in what became known as the Nine Years War. O'Neill, with the aid of many – but not all – Irish chieftains was slowly pushing back Elizabeth's armies. By 1580, their power base greatly reduced, the English imposed martial law in the nominally loyal province of Munster. Among those who could be executed were "idle persons…aiders of rebels…makers of *aqua vitae*". Spirits were clearly seen as one of the causes of unrest.

What made the situation in Ireland intolerable for the Protestant Queen Elizabeth I was O'Neill's success in getting aid from the Catholic armies of Spain. Unlike the 'old English' who arrived before the Reformation, the 'new English' were Protestant; Christendom was on fire and Europe was dividing along sectarian lines. Elizabeth I felt she had to secure Ireland, otherwise she was leaving the Realm open to a Catholic invasion. The Spanish, who had already sent a failed Armada, would next time come through Ireland. Their lines of supply now secure, they would then sweep across the narrow Irish Sea. It was something she could not allow. The fuse had been lit, religion and politics had been mixed, and over the following 400 years there would be horrific consequences for both communities.

The armies of Elizabeth of England and King Philip of Spain, backed up by O'Neill's forces, finally met not far from Cork city, on a wet day in December 1601. After all the build up, and given what was at stake, the battle was little more than a brief skirmish. The Spanish surrendered, the Irish were routed and the forces of the Crown won their most important victory in Ireland. The Gaelic order collapsed, and O'Neill and the Gaelic chiefs of Ulster fled to Europe in what became known as the Flight of the Earls. This left the province of Ulster, the area most resistant to the English crown, leaderless.

Two worlds had collided. The Irish and the English had different legal systems, culture, language and religion – they even used a different calendar. The English followed the old Julian calendar and the Irish the Gregorian as decreed by Pope Gregory XIII in 1582. With the departure of the Gaelic Lords, the way was clear for what became known as the Plantation of Ulster. Following the death of Elizabeth, this was a unique opportunity for the newly crowned James I to reward the many who had claims on his patronage.

One of those patrons was about to move into the Route in the then County of Coleraine, an area that contains the modern-day town of Bushmills.

Left: Queen Elizabeth I of England

Chapter Five

The Plantations of Ulster

The Plantation of Ulster was a planned process of colonisation. English and Scottish Protestants were given lands in parts of the counties of Donegal, Tyrone, Fermanagh, Armagh and the entirety of Coleraine. These lands had been taken from the native Irish Catholics after the Gaelic Lord Hugh O'Neill left for Europe.

The County of Coleraine no longer exists, but it was created in 1585 by Lord Deputy John Perrott, and it was situated between the rivers Bann and Foyle. Large tracts of O'Cahane's County as it had previously been known, were put under the charge of Thomas Phillips after capturing Hugh O'Neill's fort at Toome, on the shores of Lough Neagh. Phillips was described as "a very discreet and valiant commander at all times", in a book published in 1877. He picked himself out two choice parcels of land and "expanded very considerably soon after he obtained legal posession of the same". In other words, he made himself at home.

Like many of the gentry who landed in Ulster, Captain Thomas Phillips was out to feather his own nest. He acquired a twenty-one year lease on Customs into the area and the ferries on all river crossings into and out of Coleraine. In 1608 he was made a Knight of the realm and the following year he was granted the patent for *aqua vitae*.

At this time there was no whiskey industry. Everyone and anyone could distil. It was a cottage industry, and as much a part of everyday life as butter making or weaving. It was a great way of using up surplus grain. Whiskey didn't go off, it could be traded or rubbed as a cure-all or taken internally for its 'medicinal' properties.

During Tudor times it was a common and corrupt practice for the English Crown to sell monopolies. These monopolies or 'patents' were sold for just about anything – the importation of sweet wine, the brewing of beer or the distillation of whiskey. In return for either a cash payment or a proportion of the take (hence the term 'royalty'), the patent holder was given a state-guaranteed monopoly in a particular area, and in turn they could sub-let the licence for whatever rent they could extract.

Sir Arthur Chichester succeeded Perrott as Lord Deputy of Ireland, and soon after he granted his deputy, Sir Thomas Phillips, a licence to distil.

"To Sir Thomas Phillips, Knt., and such has assignes, as shall be allowed by the chiefe governor of Ireland, was granted on 20th of Apriell, in the sixt yere, licence, for the next seaven yeres, within the countie of Colrane, otherwise called O Cahanes countrey, or within the territorie called the Rowte, in co. Antrim, by himselfe or his servauntes, to make, drawe, and distill such as soe great quantities of aquavite, usquabagh and aqua composita, as he or his assignes shall thinke fitt; and the same to sell, vent, and dispose of to any persons, yeeldinge yerelie the somme 13s 4d etc; with power to sue, arrest and impleade all persons as shall make any aquavite therin, for such paines, penalties and forfeitures, as are limited in the statutes of 3rd and 4th Phillip and Marie, ch. 7, and the same to receave and convert to her or their use, without rendering any account-prohibiting all persons, etc. other than the said Sir Thomas, and his assignes, to make, distill or vent same, upon payne of imprisonment, and such fynes as by the cheife governor and counsell of Ireland shal be thought meete; provided this graunt be not prejudicall to any peers, gentlemen, burgesses, or other persons by said acte excepted; nor to any inhabitant, residinge within the liberties of the countie of Derrie; nor to any licence graunted to any persons, to make aquavite within the places before mentioned; and that this licence do cease and determine, after the expiration of one yere from the date hereof, upon notice given by the chiefe governor, yf it appear by any cause that same may prove hurtful to the commonwealth."

It is from this grant of licence to make "aquavite" dated 20th April 1608 that the Old Bushmills distillery claims its ancient heritage. Of course there was no distillery, there were no bottles of whiskey and even the date is now wrong. The British adopted the modern Gregorian calendar in 1752, which means the licence was actually issued on what today is 30th April.

By 1609 the Plantation was far from secure, and Sir Thomas Phillips went to London and met the Earl of Salisbury. Irish bandits known as 'wood-kerne' were attacking the colonies around Coleraine, and it had become difficult to find settlers. The solution arrived at was ingenious. They would approach the City of London to fund a proper Plantation.

This was not the first time the powerful London Guilds had been involved in speculative plantations. The Virginia Company of London had been established in 1606 to fund colonial settlements in North America. The City fathers were not convinced there was enough in Ireland to make it worth their while, but they agreed to visit the area, accompanied by Sir Thomas Phillips. He was told to ensure that the deputation should leave with a favourable impression, and indeed they were impressed by the vast stretches of valuable oak forest.

The Livery Companies of London reached an agreement with the King in January 1610. It was very much on their terms, and they got their hands on the entire county of Coleraine, which Sir Thomas had set his heart on clearing.

Sir Thomas Phillips was given 3,000 acres to compensate for his loss of Coleraine, and he set out a new settlement at Limavady. He was deeply unhappy with the compromise, and in 1622 he commissioned cartographer Thomas Raven to map the settlements of the London Companies. He used the maps to back up his case that the Guilds were not fulfilling their obligations. In the end Phillips returned to England and died a broken and bitter man. Perhaps he missed Coleraine too much, or maybe, just maybe, he was mourning his loss of a certain licence to make *aqua vitae* in the county of Coleraine.

Chapter Six
Modern Times

It says a lot about Old Bushmills that a section titled 'Modern Times' starts in 1610. But then, as one of the two towns developed by the London Guilds, Coleraine (the other was Londonderry – Guilds commonly added their title to 'Planted' towns) was being laid out and the Diamond in the town centre was completed in this year.

Coleraine quickly became a centre of commerce. The river Bann was the scene of great industry with limekilns, brickyards and timber stores supplying building materials for the new town. Around this time, watermills began to appear on the River Bush, and indeed the name Bushmills dates from the early 17th century.

We know precious little about what was happening in the hundreds of distilleries scattered around the country. Across much of the land, distilleries were farm based and family operated. Up until 1761 registration was voluntary, and to register meant tax had to be paid. It is easy to believe Victorian writer Alfred Barnard's account of how in 1743 distilling in the Bushmills area was "in the hands of smuggler".

It is 1766 before the tax returns for the Coleraine area, which included Bushmills, give us our first snapshot of distilling in the area. They list 45 stills as being licensed, but you can be certain there was at least that amount again unlicensed.

At this point in time distilleries were widely scattered across rural areas of the country, where there were poor transport links and the rule of law was most often observed by its absence. If keeping track of who distilled what was difficult, collecting revenue must have been even harder. Areas like Coleraine were relatively well policed, but in the West of Ireland, or in the Highlands of Scotland, the Crown had very little presence. A fortune in uncollected Excise was being lost.

In 1779 the government in London, tired of chasing distillers over the muddy highways and byways of the Celtic fringe, changed the way it would collect revenue. They imposed a duty on the still, not on the spirit it produced. The idea was to simplify duty collection and "to secure receipt of the whole licence duty without risk and almost without expense". The Crown worked out how much you owed, by estimating how much spirit you could produce if you charged a still four times in twenty-eight days. This meant that before they even started, some small operators owed more in tax than they could ever earn. Caught between the larger distilleries and the unlicensed poitín makers, these small distilleries were squeezed out of business. When the new tax regime came into force there were some 1,228 distilleries in Ireland; a year later just 246 were still registered. In the Coleraine Excise area for example 47 stills are recorded in 1782, down to only 8 by 1791. The missing distillers hadn't gone out of business – they had simply gone underground.

The year 1784 is important, because this is when a business, probably related to the distillery that exists today, was first registered as Bushmills. Indeed '1784' was embossed on bottles and printed on all Old Bushmills labels until the mid-1960s.

Chapter Seven

The Poteen Years

The decades that followed the introduction of the Still Tax in 1779 have become known as 'The Poteen Years'. Legitimate operations like the newly established Bushmills disappear from the records; these distilleries either went out of business or joined the black market.

Those whiskey makers that stayed on the right side of the law had to battle for survival. The only way they could get ahead of the Excise was to charge and recharge their stills more often than was permitted. With a fixed tax payable on the theoretical output of a still, distillers made their money by squeezing in as many extra distillations as they could. As a contemporary Excise officer put it, "no matter how good a distiller, unless he can work rapidly he would be ruined in Ireland".

This shoddily made 'Parliament whiskey' soon earned itself a bad reputation, while the reputation of carefully made, but illegal, poitín grew and grew. By 1820 the Revenue estimated that half of all the spirits consumed in the United Kingdom came from either smugglers or illicit stills.

By 1823 there were just 20 legitimate distilleries operating in Ireland. Aeneas Coffey, an Excise officer in Donegal estimated that on Ulster's Inishowen peninsula, just across a narrow stretch of water from the Coleraine Excise district, there were at least 800 illegal stills. We also know the poitín from Inishowen was being openly sold as far away as Dublin. There is even a record of 50 gallons being seized in Belfast: ironically this particular consignment came from Toomebridge on the shores of Lough Neagh, the homeland of Sir Thomas Phillips.

As American Prohibition was to show a century later, taking the manufacture and sale of alcohol out of the hands of legitimate business and driving it underground only ends in anarchy. The gangsters of 19th-century Ireland were in equal parts ruthless and clever. These 'moonshiners' were heavily armed, and vicious running battles with Excise were commonplace. During one of these clashes the aforementioned Coffey suffered a cracked skull and had a bayonet plunged twice through his thigh. He survived to become Inspector General of Excise. Others however weren't so lucky. As another Excise man, G.E. Howard, wrote:

"Revenue officers are frequently assaulted, wounded and sometimes killed in the execution of their duty".

By the end of 1823 it was clear that the government had got it very wrong. The old Still Tax was dropped and from now on distillers only paid duty on what they produced. The effect was drastic and immediate. In 1821 there were just 32 licensed whiskey makers in the land, mushrooming to 93 by 1835.

proceeds were then divided up among shareholders and creditors. The Inspector of Taxes suspected this was not tax avoidance, which is legal – this was tax evasion, which is not. They felt the company was trading, and they wanted their tax on the profits of whiskey sold up to April 1921. This case went as far as the House of Lords and in the end the Revenue lost. By 1923 the distillery was back on the market and up for sale in a very different Ireland.

Left: The old bridge over the River Bush and water mills, early 1900s

Above: The distillery in the early 1900s. The twin pagoda roofs are conspicuous by their absence. On the left, St Columb's Rill flows towards the dam, past the 'modern' multi-storey warehouse n°2.

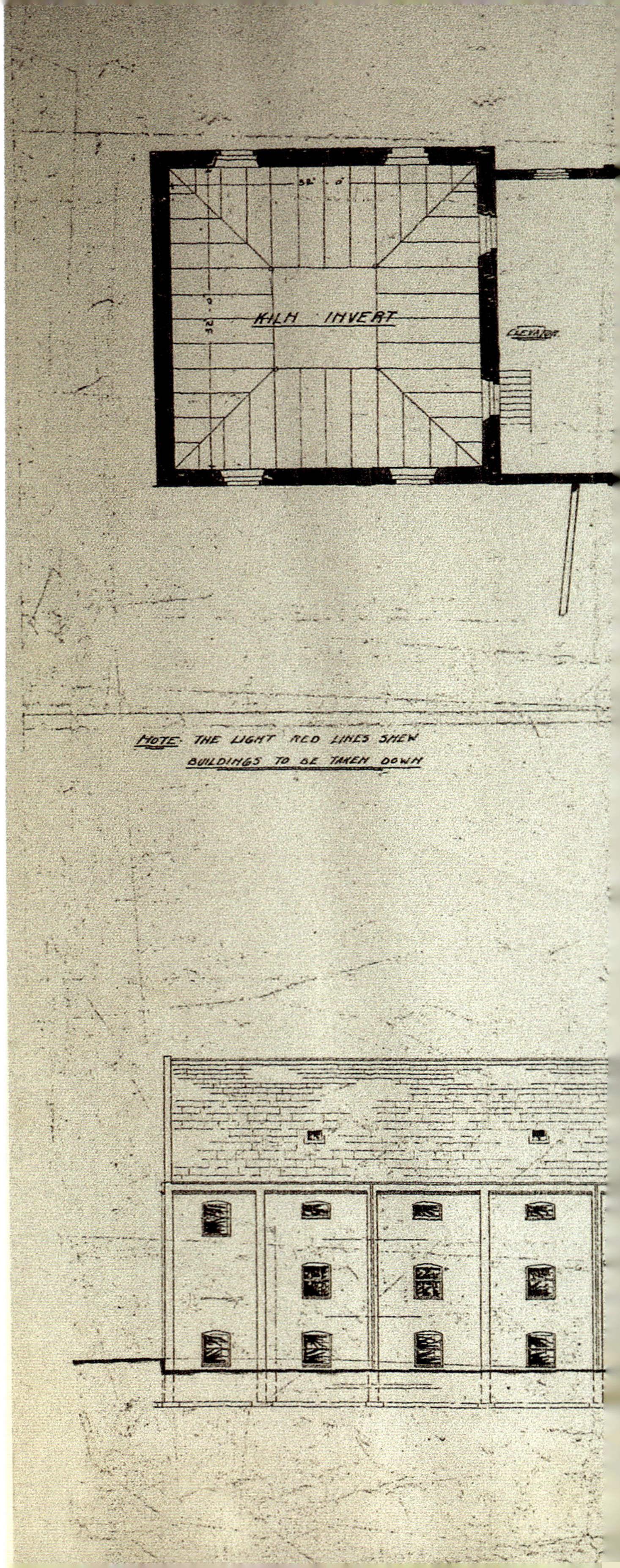

Right: The distillery's malting floors and kilns, with their remarkable pagoda roofs, were a relatively late addition to Bushmills, designed by Victorian distillery architect Charles C. Doig in 1910. They accommodated Allied Forces servicemen stationed in Bushmills during the War and even produced malted barley for Guinness. On-site malting was abandoned in the early 1970s and they now host the visitors' café and shop.

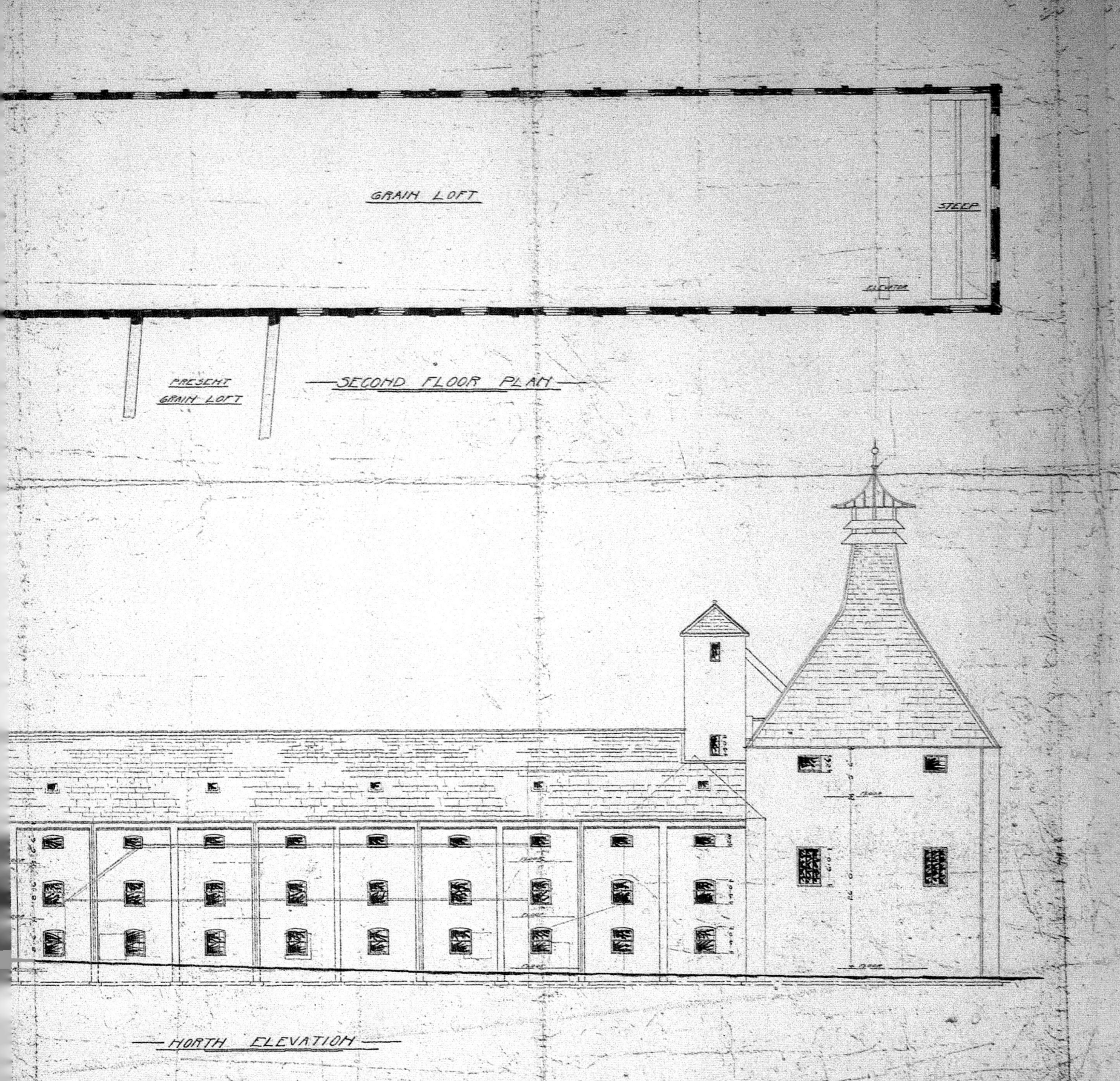

Right: An illustration showing the newly installed pagoda roofed malting floors and kilns

Chapter Sixteen

Partition

On a clear day it is possible to stand on the North Antrim coast and gaze across the distance at Scotland. A millennium and more ago all this was part the Gaelic kingdom of *Dalriada*. The people who lived on both sides of the narrow Irish Sea were called *Scotti*; it is the origin of the word 'Scotland', though it means 'inhabitants of Ireland'.

Both populations cross-pollinated again when Scottish Protestants came to live in the north of Ireland after the Plantation of Ulster. Over the years thousands of people have drifted over and back, trading barley, picking potatoes or fishing. The Act of Union 1800 finally brought the Kingdom of Ireland into political union with Scotland, England and Wales to create the United Kingdom of Great Britain and Ireland. But it was an unstable union. The majority of Catholics on the southern part of the island wanted Home Rule, something most Protestant Unionists dismissed as 'Rome Rule', as they feared the influence the Catholic Church would gain if the Union were dissolved.

The General Election of 1918 then was pivotal. It took place against the backdrop of the Great War. The Republican Easter Rising in Dublin of two years earlier was important as it led to a unilateral declaration of Irish independence. However, the Anglo-Irish Treaty of 1921 allowed Northern Ireland to opt out of the Irish Free State, which it did and this led to the partition of the island. There were now two Home Rule Parliaments, one in Dublin the other in Belfast.

The fracturing of the Union was to have an unforeseen effect on the manufacture of whiskey. In 1922 there were 16 distilleries on the island, with 5 in Northern Ireland. Up until this point the same laws applied to Irish and Scotch whisky, thereafter the Irish Free State went its own way, leaving the distilleries that lay north of the border under Crown rule.

The newly independent Free State had a love-hate attitude to whiskey. On one hand it wanted to enhance the reputation of its pot-still whiskey, so it increased the

Left: Partition divided Ireland in two.

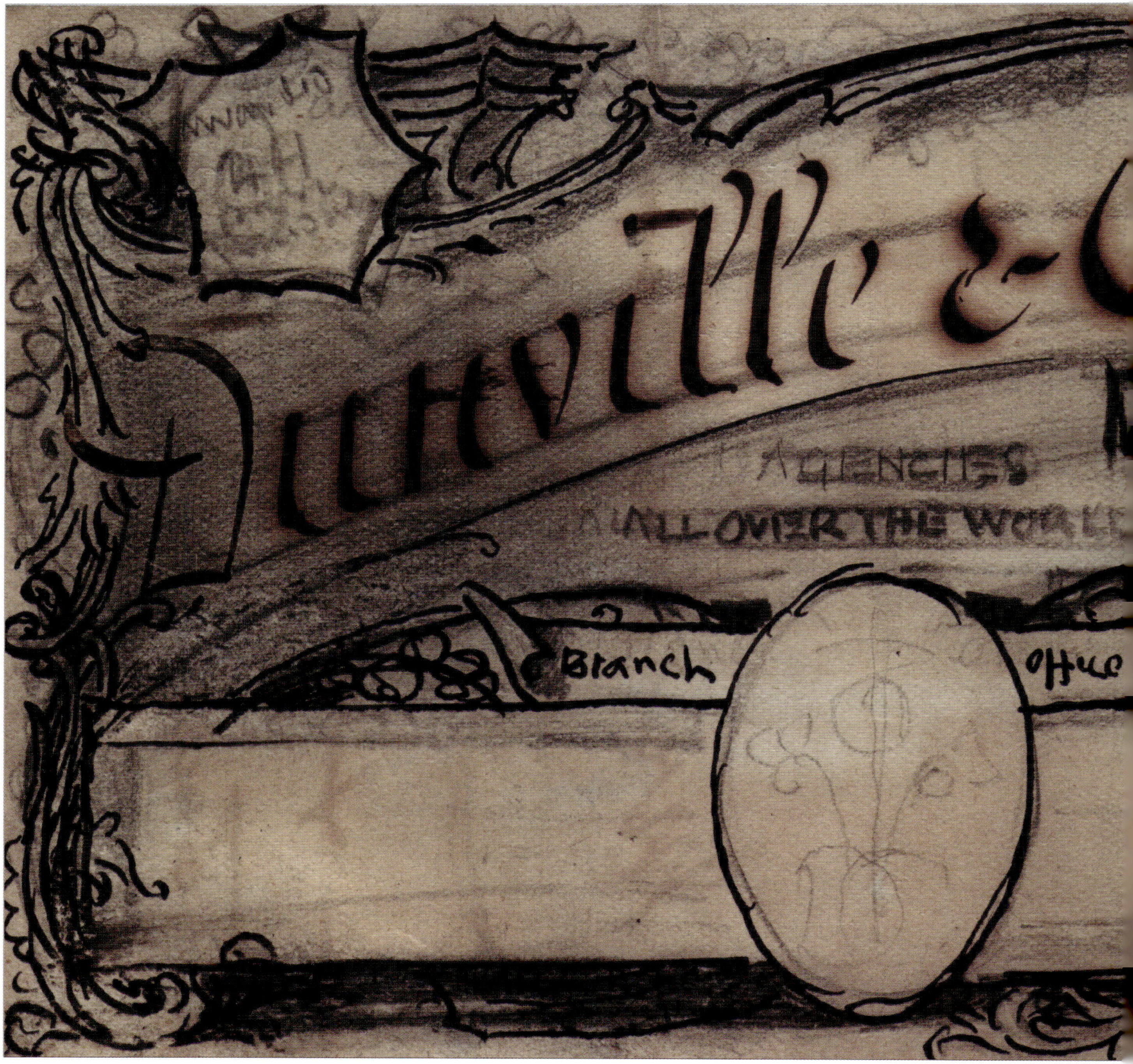
AGENCIES
ALL OVER THE WORLD
Branch

minimum time whiskey had to be matured from three to five years. On the other hand Ernest Blythe, the first Minister for Finance labelled the country's distillers "the dregs of landlordism". Blythe was referring to people like Andrew Jameson, a Senator, a Protestant and the fifth generation of Jameson to run the Dublin distillers, who also happened to be a staunch Unionist, and Sir John Power, who quietly dropped the 'Sir' and the Royal warrant after independence. This underlying nationalism meant there was no real interest in helping the "Unionist industry". The Free State government was caught between a worldwide swing towards conservative temperance and their need for the industry as "a source of very substantial revenue".

For a different set of reasons, the whiskey business north of the border didn't fare much better. By 1922 the mighty Ulster distilleries of Derry's Waterside and Abbey Street, as well as Belfast's Connswater and Avoniel had been taken over and shut down. By 1929 there were just one grain plant and three small pot distilleries left in Ulster – one of these was Old Bushmills.

Left: A mock-up for Dunville Whiskey. Dunville's Royal Irish Distillery in Belfast was one of three which still survived in Ulster in the early 1930s.

FOUR HUNDRED YEARS IN THE MAKING | 69

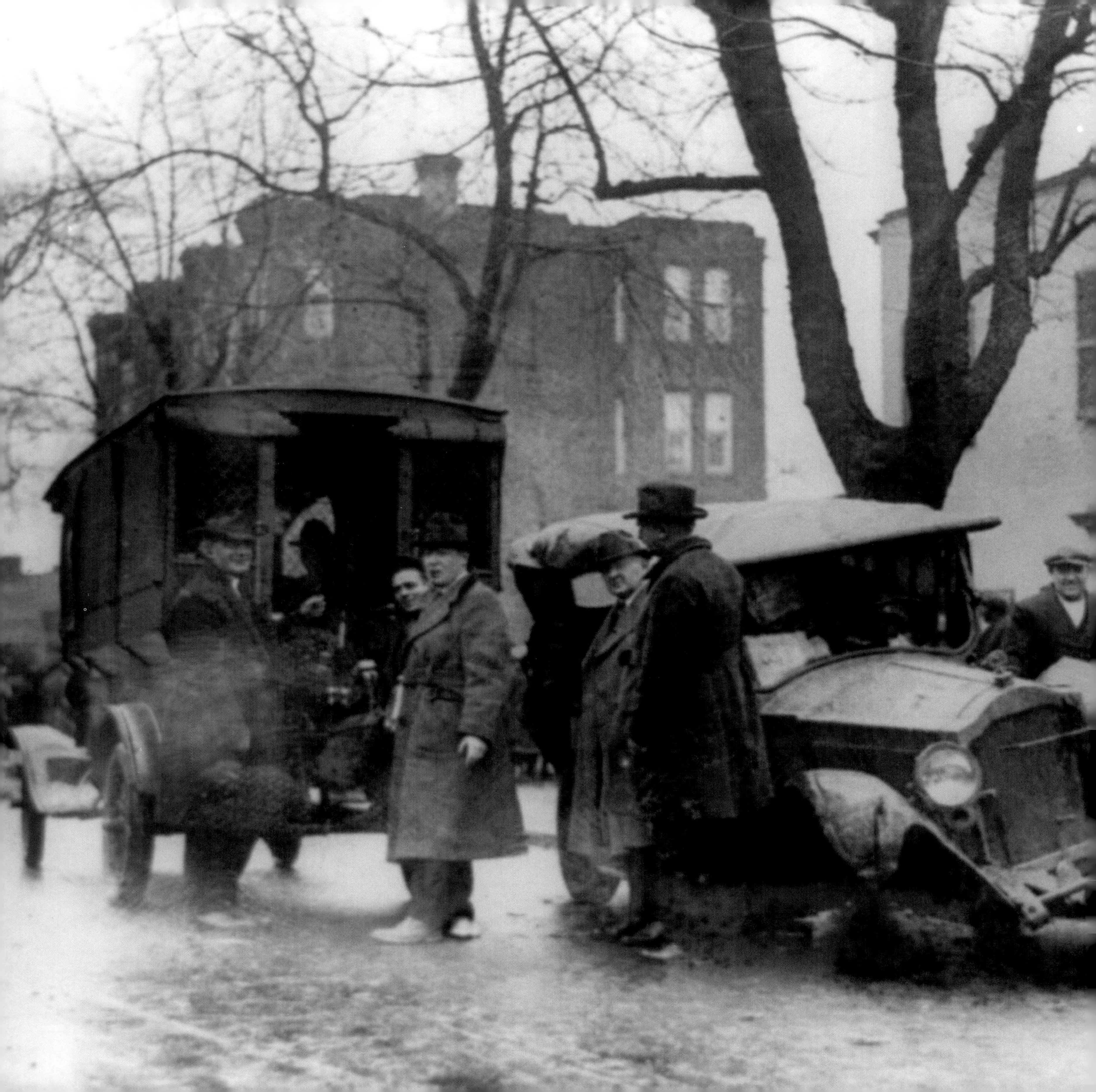

Chapter Seventeen
The Noble Experiment

Nowadays the word 'prohibition' has become synonymous with 1920s America. But in the early decades of the 20th century, a wave of anti-drink zeal gripped Western Europe. Many countries including Russia, Iceland and Norway prohibited the sale of alcohol. Lloyd George told the UK that "we are fighting Germany, Austria and drink, and the greatest of these deadly foes is drink."

The United Kingdom then came very close to banning alcohol. In 1916 *The New York Times* ran a major story under the headline 'Prohibition Wave Sweeping Britain'. The article explained that the King had banned alcohol throughout his household but "the impression is growing that the Government will content itself with bringing in a measure prohibiting the sale of spirits." The newspaper was right – in the end, Britain opted for control over Prohibition. Pub opening hours were shortened and they had to close in mid-afternoon, which in Ireland became known as "the holy hour".

In the United States, Prohibition started out as a realisation of the American Dream. The Volstead Act of 1919 prohibited the "manufacture, sale, or transportation of intoxicating liquors" but what happened next was unexpected. The manufacture, sale and transportation of intoxicating liquors went from the hands of legitimate business into the hands of gangsters. Irish whiskey, prized and sold at a premium in pre-Prohibition American, was an obvious target for the bootleggers, who wasted no time in producing their own version of Irish whiskey. This bootlegging caused huge and lasting damage to the reputation of Irish whiskey in the States.

Prohibition meant that from the middle of January 1920, the vast market of the United States of America was closed to Irish and Scottish whiskey exporters. Almost immediately distilleries across these islands were mothballed: the English whiskey industry would never recover. However, there was

Left: After a chase through the streets of Washington, some bootleggers are apprehended by the Capitol Police (1921)

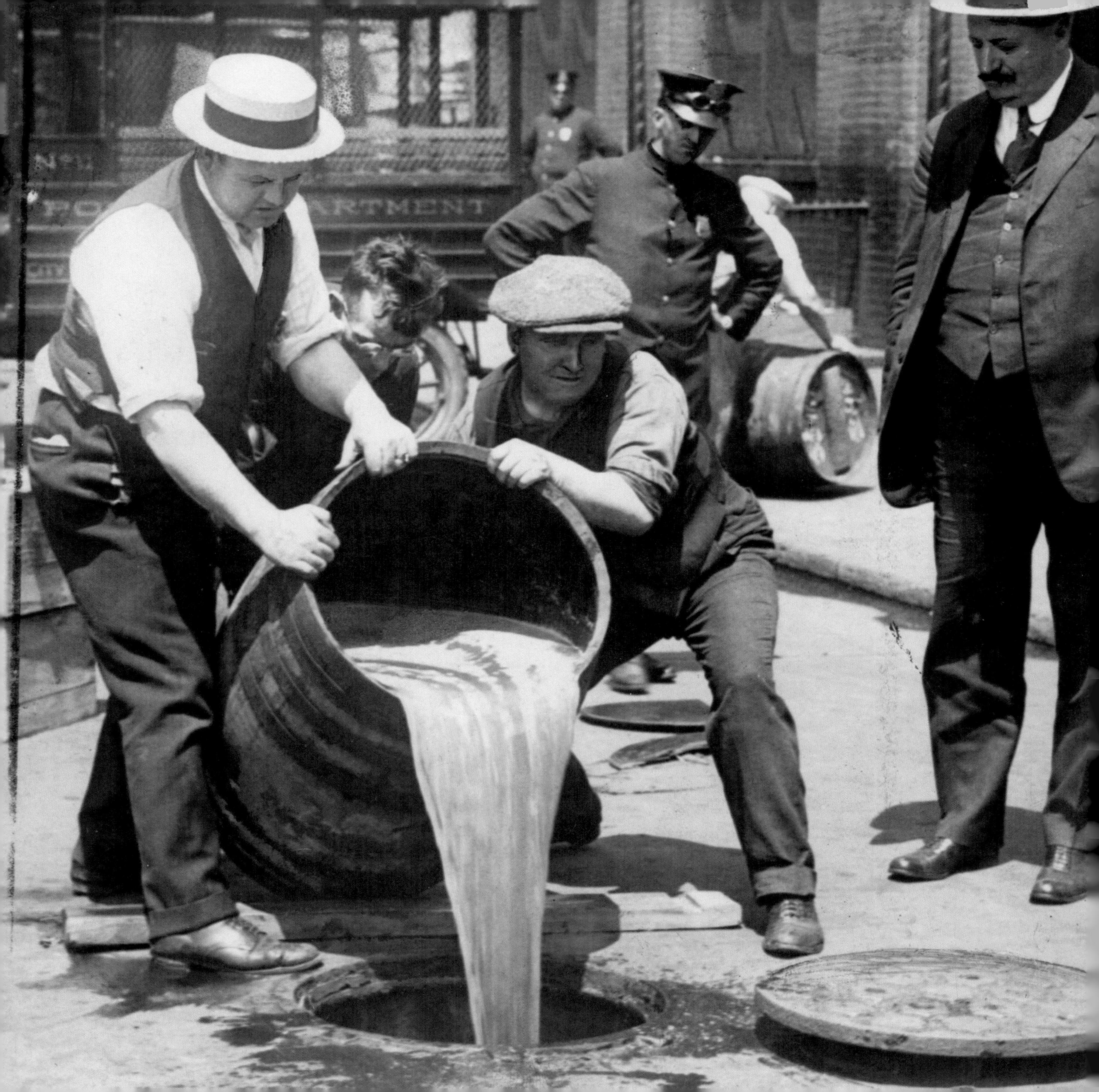

a loophole that allowed spirits to be sold through registered pharmacies for medicinal purposes. The Scots quickly cornered this market with their single malts and blends.

At the height of the 'dry' season in 1923, the Rudd brothers created the 'Cutty Sark' blend specifically for the American market. Their new whisky was shipped to the Bahamas, then loaded aboard British registered vessels which anchored in international waters off New York, in what became known as 'Rum Row'. Sometimes it was smuggled in through Canada, where it found a welcome market. Within a couple of decades 'Cutty Sark' was the biggest selling Scotch in the United States.

While Capone and his ilk were destroying the reputation of Irish whiskey, and the Scots were busy building brands in America, the major Irish distillers were sleepwalking towards disaster. In the 1920s Joe Kennedy (father of John F. Kennedy), approached both Jameson and Powers with a speculative 'post-Prohibition' order for whiskey. Even though both companies could have done with the work they declined, as accepting the business would be conniving to break the law. Joe Kennedy then approached the Scots, who had no problem filling his order.

The Irish, with one honourable exception, simply turned their backs on the closed American market. That exception was Samuel Wilson Boyd, and he had recently bought himself a distillery – Old Bushmills.

Left: John A. Leach, Deputy Police Commissioner for New York, watches agents pour liquor into sewer following a raid in 1921

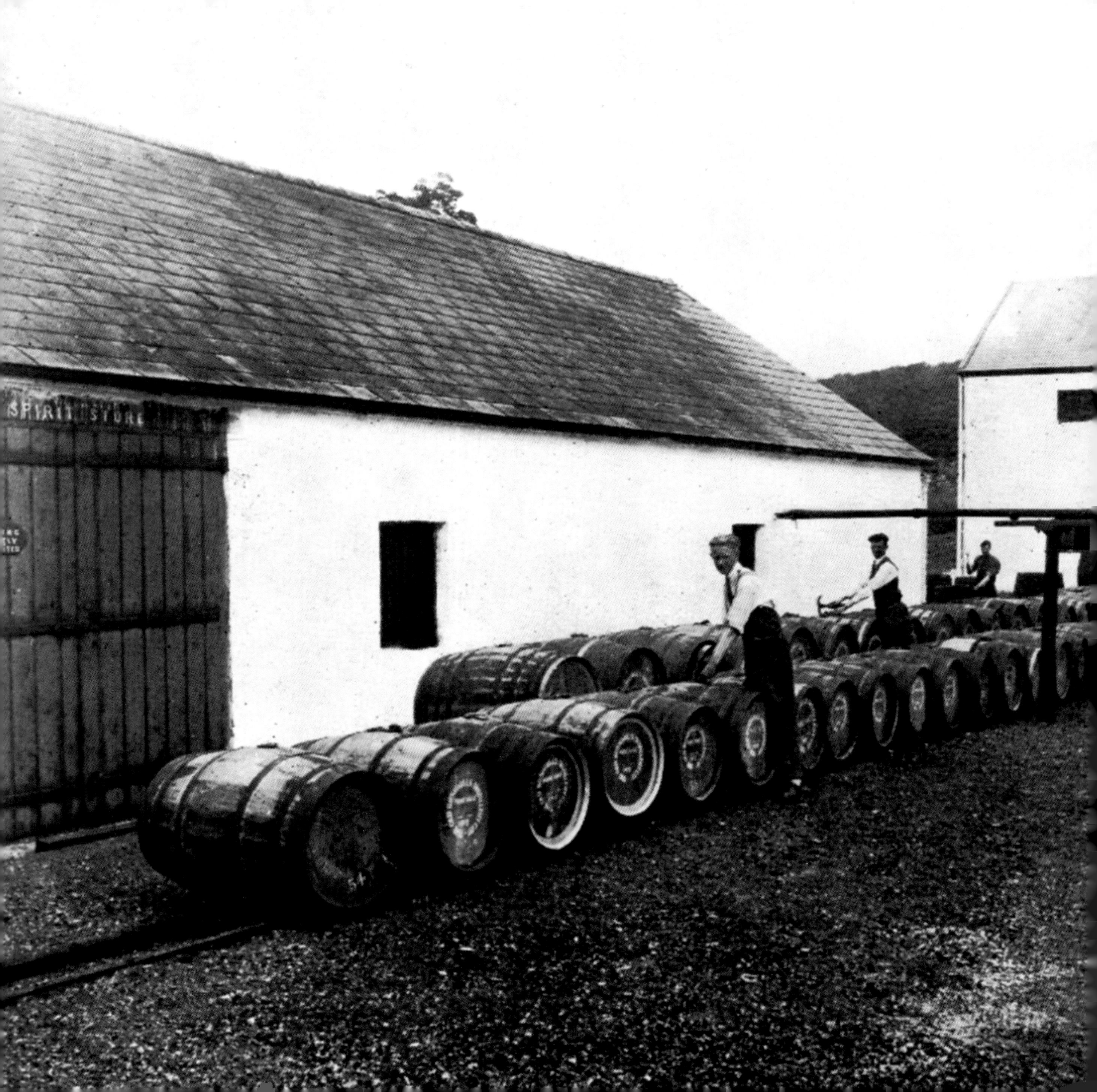
SPIRIT STORE

Chapter Eighteen

Ireland's Best

In the days before distillery-bottled whiskeys like 'Black Bush', most Irish distillers stuck to making the whiskey, leaving the bottling, branding and selling to somebody else. Every town had a Wine and Spirit merchants, a company who bulk bought everything from Guinness, to whiskey, to port and sold it on by the bottle. Messrs Boyd and Company of Belfast were just such a company, and their brands like 'Inishbawn' were available right across the Province and beyond.

Samuel Wilson Boyd was a self-made man, a father of fourteen children, and a strict Presbyterian of whom it has been said "he would have been a teetotal if it had not been for his business". Some time towards the start of the 20th century, Boyd established his "rectifying distillers, wine and spirit merchants" with offices in Hill Street Belfast. By all accounts he did well out of it, and sometime around 1923 he bought into Old Bushmills Distillery. It was 1930 before Boyd registered the distillery as a limited company, but thanks to a magazine article, we can clearly see that Boyd was already carving out a niche market for his whiskey.

In July 1926, *The New Era Illustrated* promised "original reviews on all matters of educational interest". Alongside stories on the making of paper, facts about anthracite and "the craze for pleating" it published an illustrated and illuminating article on 'Ireland's Best…' The magazine was published in London, but it tackled the Prohibition question head on.

"At the risk of shocking the feelings of those of our readers who applaud and uphold total abstinence, we unhesitatingly affirm that real good whiskey is one of the blessings of life."

With echoes of the 1904 World's Fair pamphlet, the article acknowledged there was a confusion about what whiskey was made from, perhaps due in no small part to bootlegging.

"Ask a person under this misconception what he – or more often than not she – thinks whiskey is made of. They will not

Left: The coopers' yard, 1926

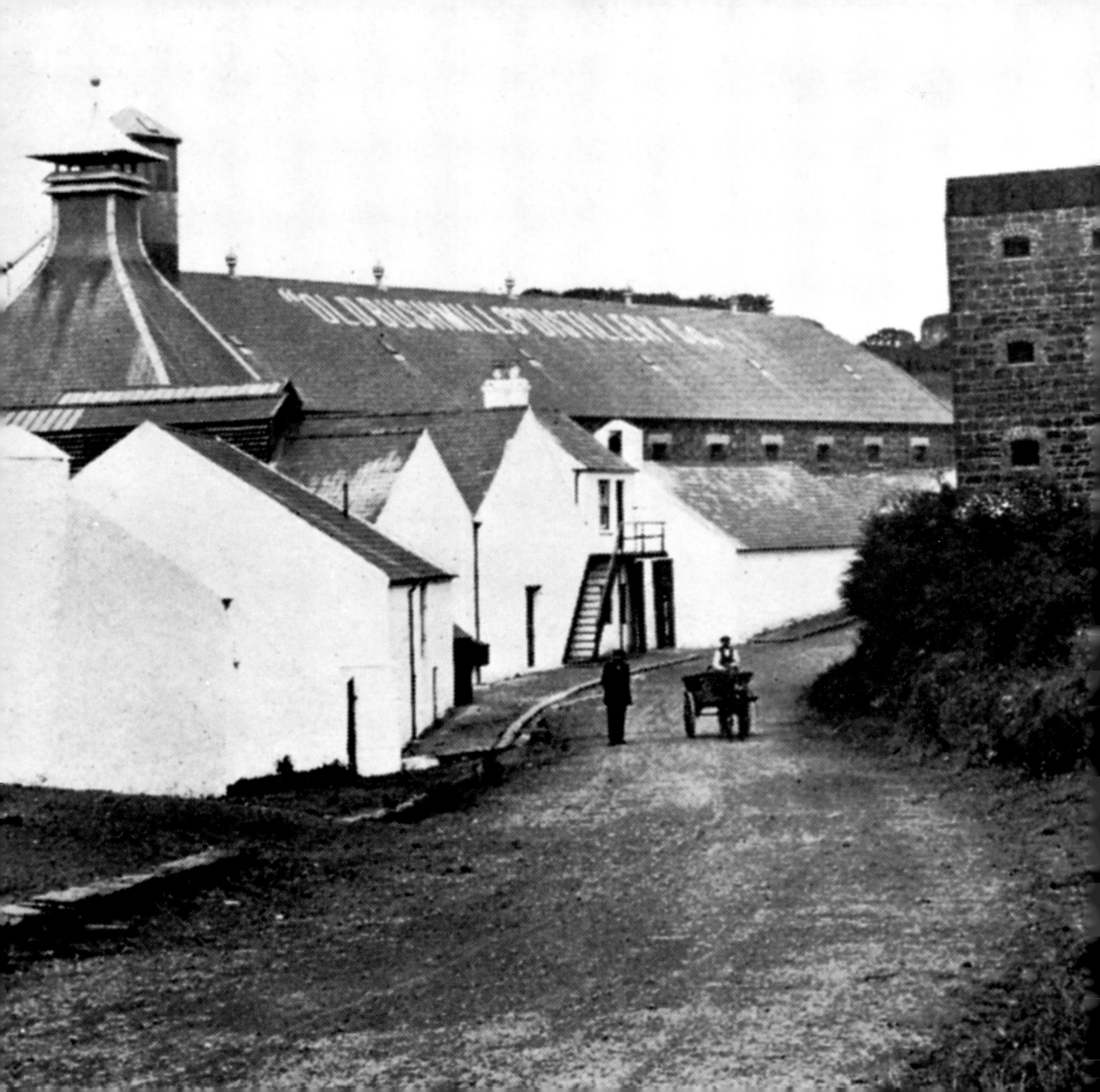

be able to answer, but they will be quite prepared to believe that its composition includes cocaine, belladonna, opium and any other vicious substances one may like to suggest."

The magazine then assures us:

"[Old Bushmills whiskey is] the old-fashioned kind which produces the best quality of whiskey, and is far superior to the patent still process."

The article paints quite a picture of the North Antrim facility, stating that "the distillery is among the most modern and up-to-date in Ireland". It continues with an inch by inch inventory of the buildings, before confirming that the plant is capable of "distilling 6,000 gallons per week…with a storage capacity of almost a million gallons."

All this was perhaps a bit overstated, as at the time Old Bushmills was mothballed and was not in production. Such coverage says a lot about Samuel Wilson Boyd's ability to sell. A similar story appeared a year later in the periodical *The Brewer*, while adverts were published in numerous local and regional publications, from football programmes to theatre bills. The adverts informed us:

"The moderate use of a good whiskey, such as Old Bushmills, is a powerful aid in retaining good health and warding off the attacks of seasonal ailments."

By the late 1920s 'Old Bushmills Liqueur Whiskey' was selling well, there was even a fifteen-year-old 'Black Bush'. During this period then it is clear that Boyd focused on sales, even appointing agents in places as diverse as Egypt and India, but he was simply selling off his stocks of mature whiskey. Perhaps Boyd needed the cash flow or perhaps his poor health prevented him from addressing the question of what to do with the distillery, which at best was in operation only intermittently. But it was 1931 before he

Left: The Distillery entrance, 1926

FOUR HUNDRED YEARS IN THE MAKING | 77

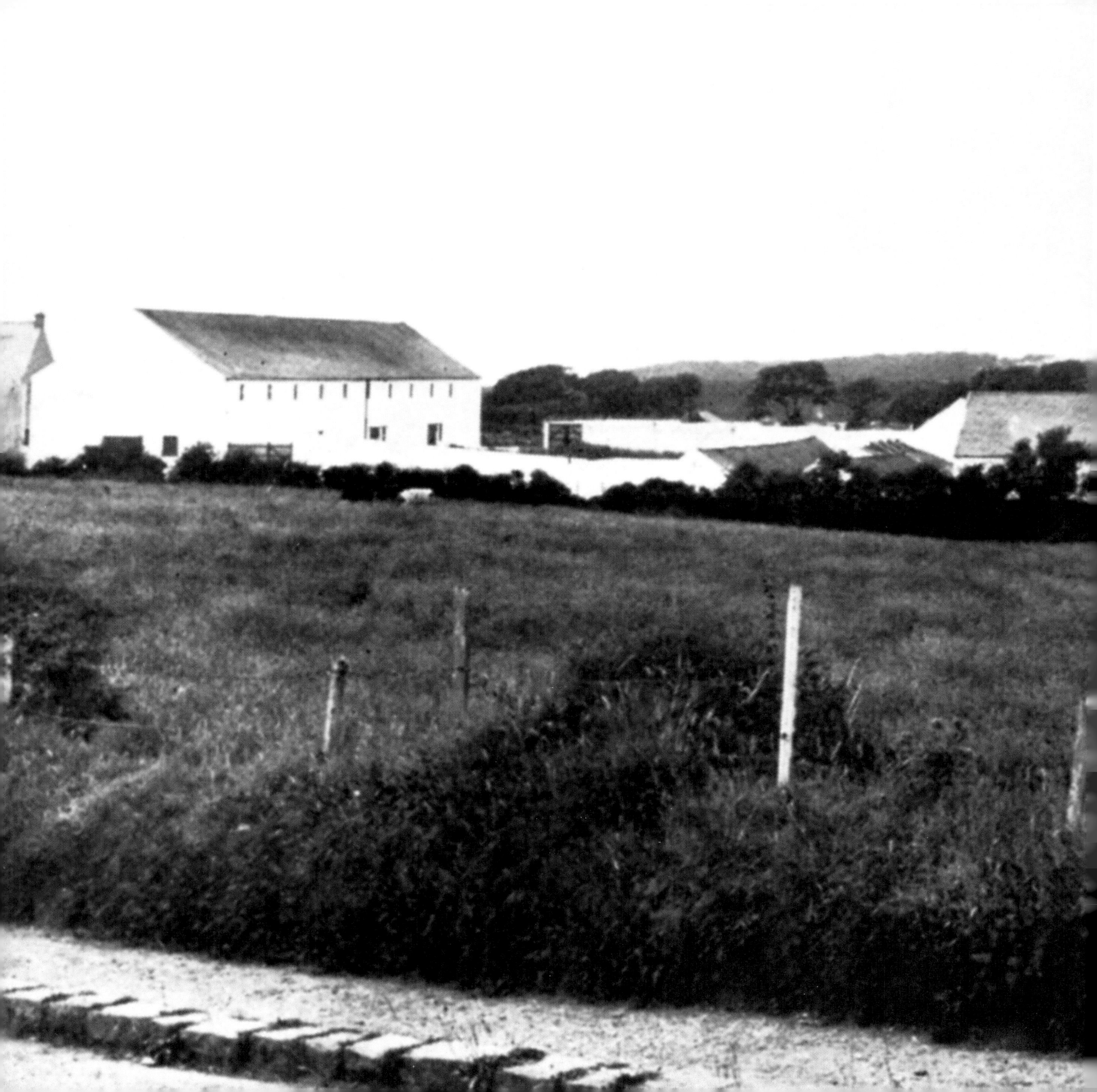

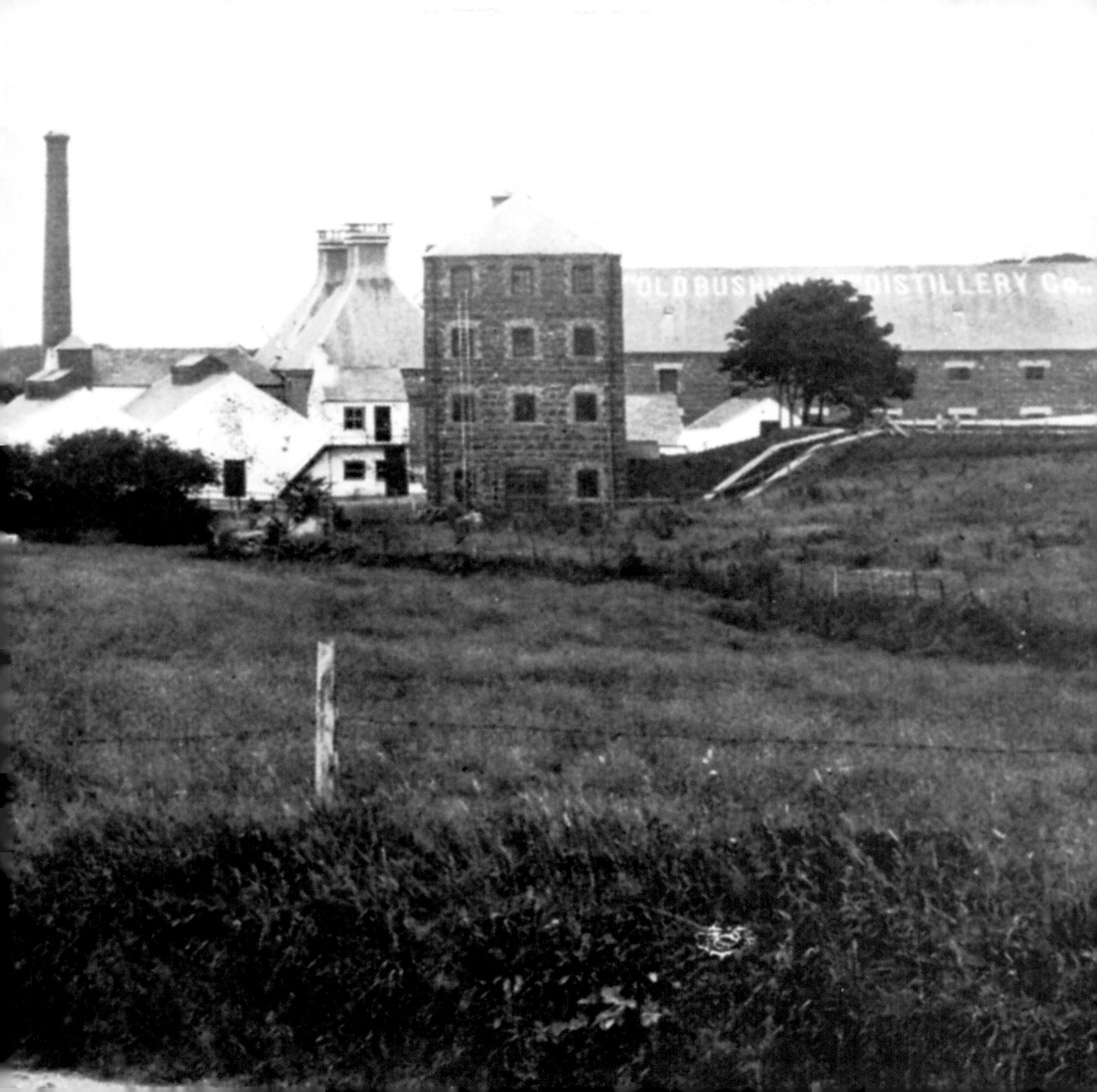
OLD BUSHM
DISTILLERY Co.

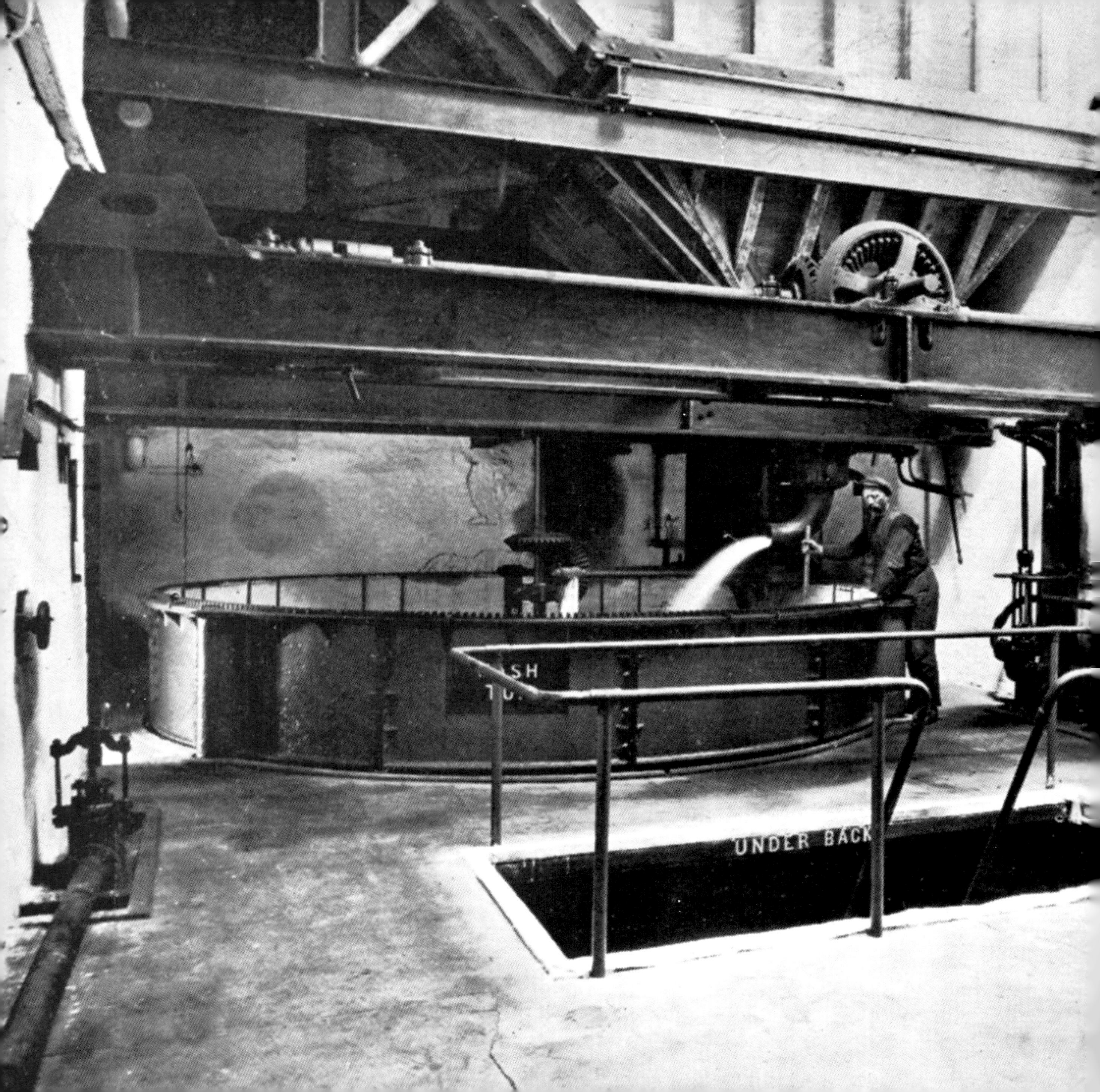
UNDER BACK

addressed the looming crisis by appointing a new manager to run Old Bushmills. The following year Samuel Wilson Boyd died of lung cancer.

In October 1929 the American stock market crashed and the world was plunged into an economic Depression. In the Irish Free State, Kilbeggan and Tullamore distilleries pulled down the shutters. They briefly re-opened only to close again by the early 1950s. To survive, even the once invincible firms of Jameson and Power in Dublin had to devalue their shares by 25% and 50% respectively. By the early 1930s the Midleton plant, with the largest pot still in the world, was distilling for two brief weeks a year.

In Northern Ireland, Dunville's Royal Irish Distillery in Belfast was the only substantial distillery left in the Province. Unbelievably, while still making a profit, the company simply gave up. In 1936, with the loss of 400 jobs, the company closed down. It would never reopen. This was one of the darkest periods in the history of whiskey making in Ireland. There were now just three tiny pot-still companies in Ulster: Old Bushmills, Upper Comber and Coleraine. But the Bushmills distillery had been more or less mothballed since 1923, its stocks of mature whiskey were very low and the owner Samuel Wilson Boyd had just died. It wasn't looking good for Bushmills, and of the three remaining Ulster distilleries, it was in by far the best shape. For a while it looked as if whiskey making, in this most historic part of Ireland, might die out completely.

Left: Inside the mash house, 1926. Note the open-top mash tun where the ground barley is mixed with hot water, and the stairs leading to the underback, the receiver where the resulting liquid (wort) is collected.

FOUR HUNDRED YEARS IN THE MAKING | 81

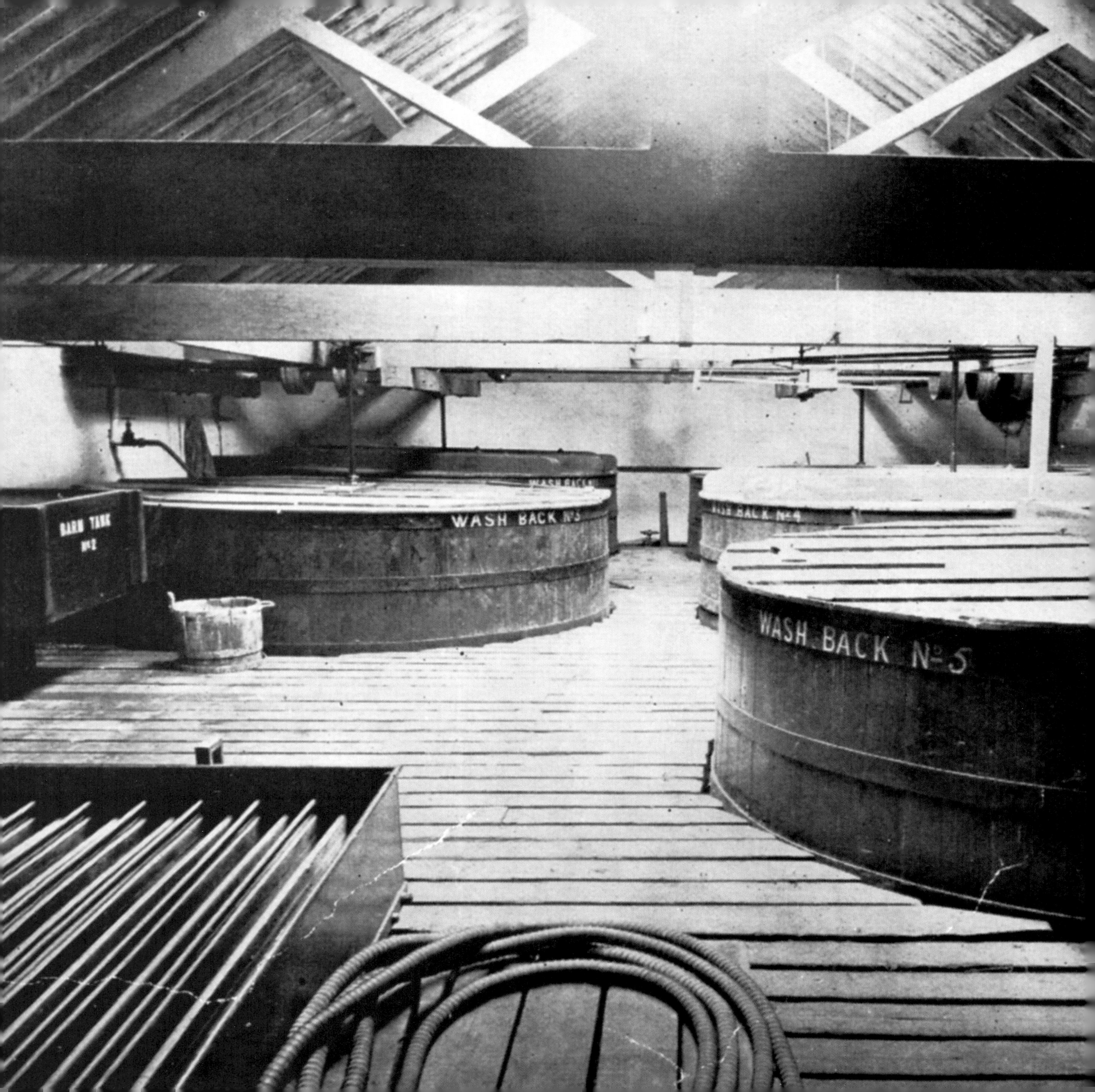
WASH BACK No. 3
WASH BACK No. 5

Chapter Nineteen

The Brothers Boyd

Following the death of his father, Wilson Boyd took over the reins at Old Bushmills. His brother Austin assisted him and together they would guide the distillery through the bleakest, leanest years of its existence. It is pretty clear that the brothers Boyd did not inherit the gleaming distillery we know today; in fact until just before his death, their father had let the place pretty much rot. A true picture of the mess they had inherited can be seen through the journal of their recently appointed Manager, James Watt Morrison.

Morrison, a taciturn Scot who had trained at DCL Mortlach distillery, was appointed in 1931. He recalls the catalogue of disasters that greeted him. The boiler "was really ancient," the floor of the Mash Tun was "in a terrible state," and the Wash Backs were so full of holes they "could not have kept in small potatoes".

Production capacity was nothing like the 6,000 gallons a week boasted of only five years previously, it was actually just short of 10,000 gallons a year. The reason that Samuel Wilson Boyd had employed the Scot quickly became clear. The distillery had run out of whiskey, Morrison discovered.

"Stocks of matured spirit amounted to a few hundred casks most of it going back to 1914."

Morrison's recollections are a remarkable insight into how Old Bushmills distillery, which on the surface at least was doing well, was in reality so close to total collapse. As he bluntly puts it: "Bushmills when I took over was not capable of operating."

The Boyds wanted to get the distillery back up and running as quickly as possible. With very little stock remaining, a very ambitious target of 30,000 gallons was set for the first year, so Morrison got to work. He bought barley direct from local farmers and dried it on the Bushmills kiln. Then the Wash Backs were mended and a Belfast shipyard copper worker came from Belfast to fix the stills. But it is clear there had

Left: The wooden wash backs (fermenting vessels) where the wort is converted into a strong beer (wash), 1926

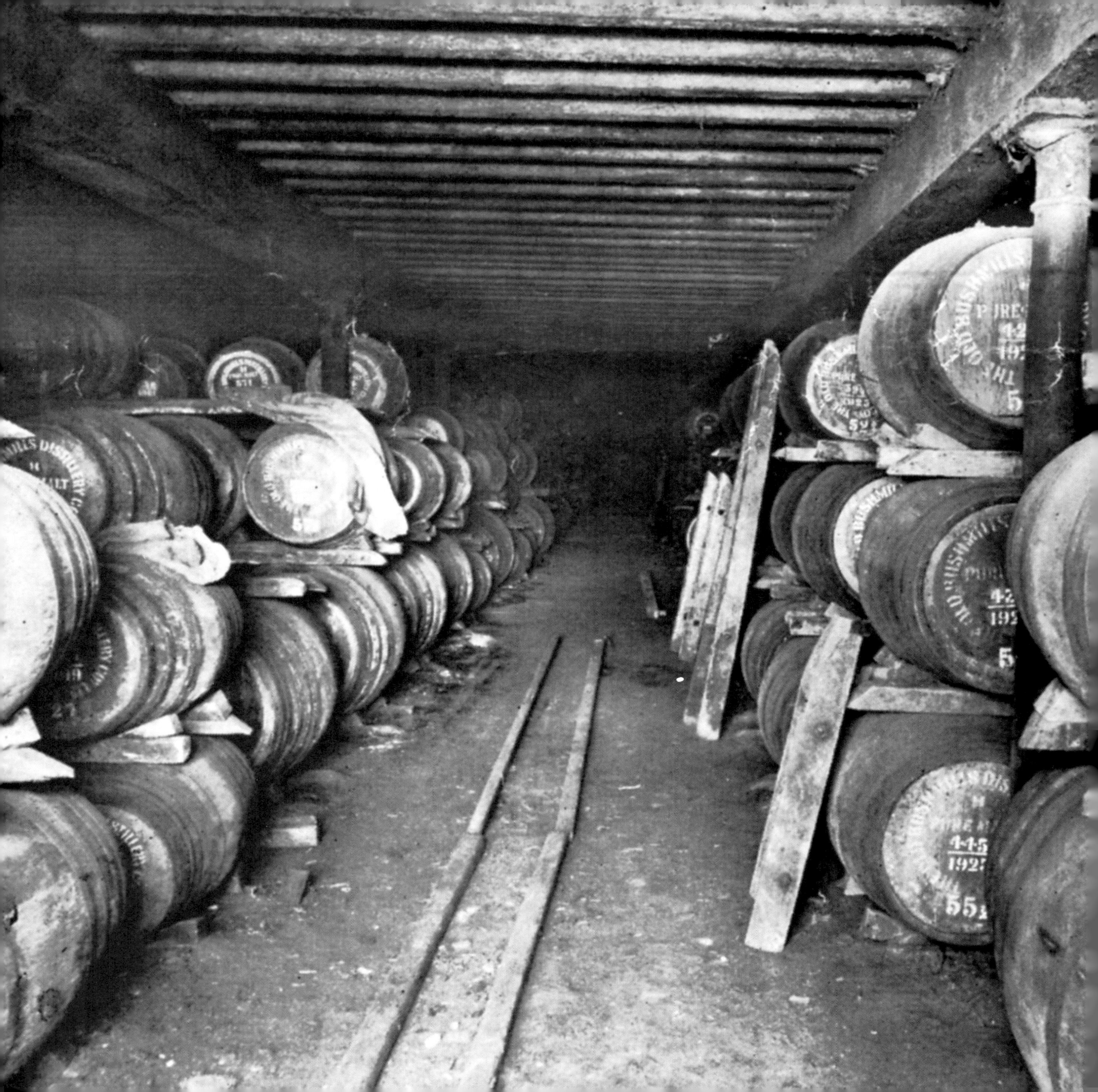

been no investment for years. No sooner had one problem been fixed than another cropped up. The list of problems goes on and on, from over-worked staff to the corn mill:

"The miller, Jim Watters told me that it very often exploded in the elevator and this I could readily believe, there was no explosion vents and the elevator was going the wrong way. The elevator had had several such accidents so that the tower was nearly two feet off plumb."

Despite everything, in mid-January 1932 the team at Old Bushmills were ready to fire up the old pot stills. Morrison's tenacity had paid off, but he would need all the resolve he could muster as the initial run of spirit was, in his own words "vile". Wilson Boyd was present for the distillation and was told in no uncertain terms that the spirit was unusable. But Morrison had a solution.

"I outlined what was in my head," he wrote, "and asked his permission to put it into practice. I immediately obtained this and so was born a triple type of pot still, not in use anywhere else."

For all the detail in Morrison's journal, he doesn't let emotion get in the way of practical information, so there no knowing what was going through his head when three weeks later the stills were fired for a second time. He simply records "we were now producing a very nice spirit". He does however allow himself the luxury of putting the statement in bold type. But we can gather from Wilson Boyd's reaction to the new make spirit, that the Scot was being self-deprecating. Boyd had been so impressed with the spirit that he took samples

Left: One of the maturation warehouses, filled with Sherry butts, 1926. Note the distilled date (1905) on one exceptionally old cask in the foreground.

FOUR HUNDRED YEARS IN THE MAKING | 85

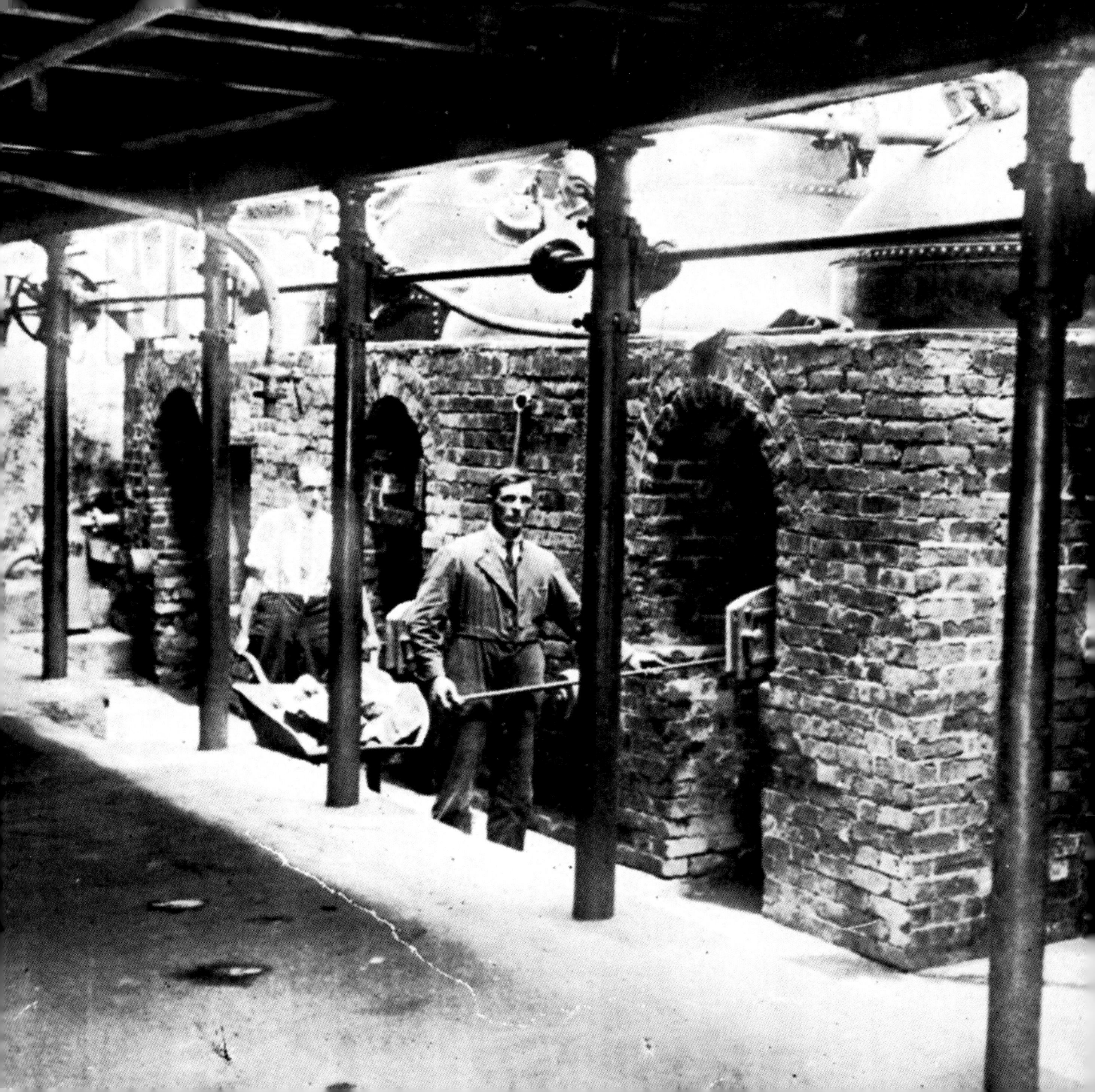

to Scotland, where they received an enthusiastic response. Morrison was offered a pay rise and asked if he could increase production. He recalls that after discussing matters with Wilson Boyd "the quality of the present standard was not expected by himself or his brothers".

We can tell from Morrison's memoirs that the Boyd brothers knew little about the practical day-to-day running of a distillery and at every turn they sought and took advice from colleagues in Scotland. But it is clear they knew Old Bushmills was a distillery living on past glories, that they needed to secured its future and set it on track for future glory. But along with the money, the Boyd brothers had the will to make things happen. Within two seasons the distillery workforce had increased to eleven, while output had gone up tenfold to some 100,000 gallons a year.

It takes three years to turn new make spirit into Irish whiskey. However, this is a bare minimum, a legal requirement, and whiskey is not bottled at three years and a day. More often than not it takes five to seven years for a whiskey to have matured enough to be blended. A single malt from Bushmills though can be a decade or two old before it is ready to be enjoyed. By the mid-1930s, although Old Bushmills was again making whiskey, none of it was saleable. With their warehouses now emptier than ever, Wilson Boyd bought up the stock of the well-respected, but mothballed, Comber distillery as well as some mature grain whiskey from the closed Belfast plant Avoniel. These whiskies, along with what little Old Bushmills whiskey remained were blended and sold under a variety

Left: Inside the still house, 1926. Men stoking the coal-fired furnaces heating the stills. Note the riveted stills.

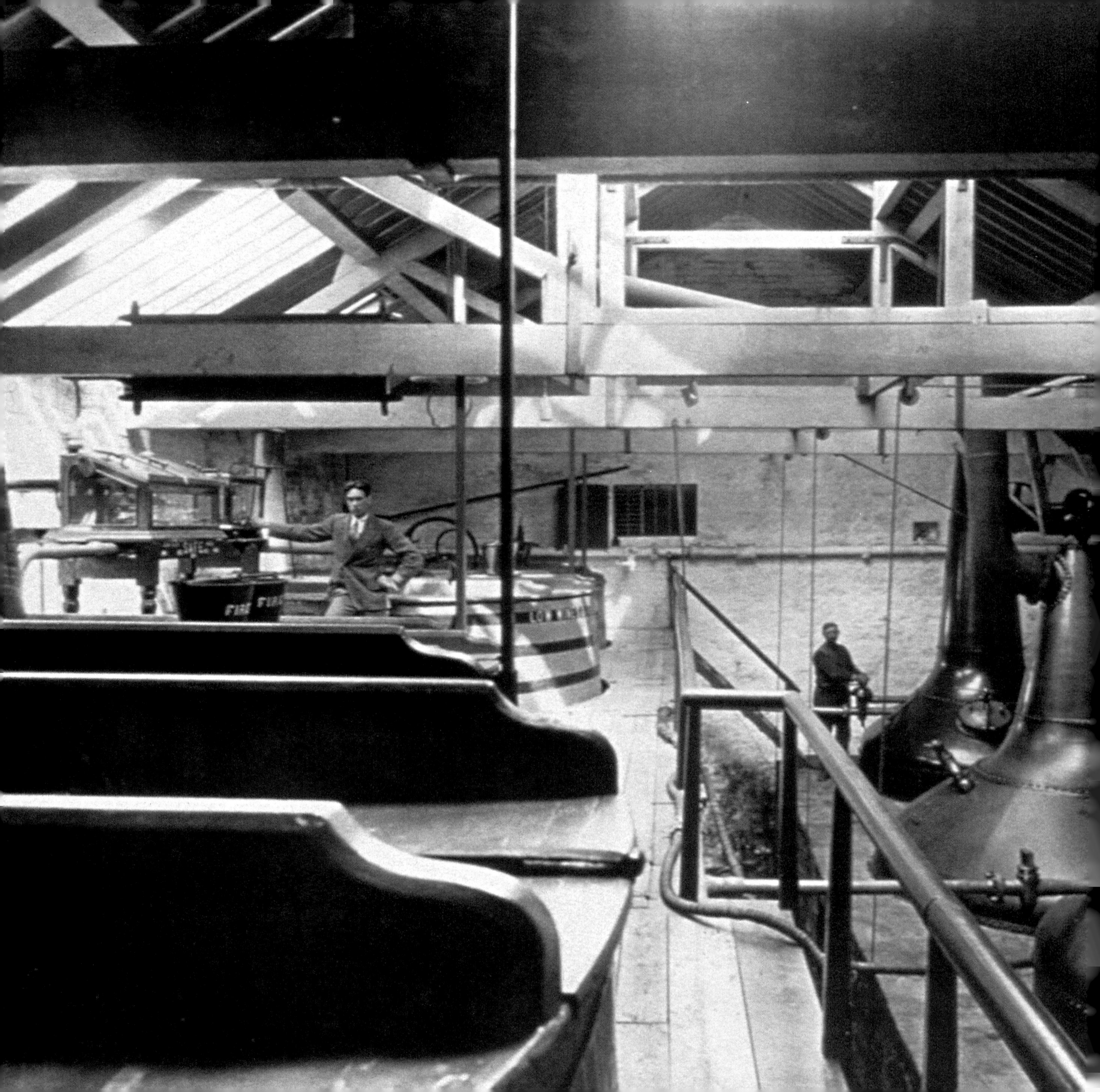

of Boyd-owned labels. Without this cash flow the company couldn't have survived. Maturing whiskey for a decade or more plays havoc with cash flow: what other business produces something, then locks it up for a decade before selling it? It takes very deep pockets to start up a distillery, and in essence that is what Wilson Boyd was doing.

Despite the poor condition of the distillery and the collapse of the domestic whiskey market, Old Bushmills was buzzing with activity. The Boyds were in this for the long haul. They were investing heavily in production and were cannily looking around to buy more mature whiskey. What they found hit the headlines of the *Belfast News Letter* on 7th September 1933. 'Belfast Firm's Purchase' ran the story of how the Coleraine distillery had just been bought by Messrs Boyd and Co. Whatever about it being a "local transaction", the writer clearly saw the commercial reasons for Wilson Boyd's interest.

"Recent events in the United States in regard to the voting on the liquor question have been closely followed by interests in Europe likely to be affected by the result."

On the same day *The New York Times* reported that "the Coleraine company, more than a decade old, has enormous stocks of bonded liquor". Indeed it had, and that paper added another interesting piece of information; Wilson Boyd had "recently returned from New York."

On 5th December 1933 President Franklin D. Roosevelt repealed the Volstead Act, bringing an end to Prohibition. After his broadcast to the nation he allegedly said, "I think that this would be a good time to have a beer."

It turned out that Boyd the canny businessman had pulled off quite a coup, so it is not surprising that he was reported to be "highly pleased" with his purchase of Coleraine. Following the repeal of Prohibition, the Irish whiskey industry was in no shape to cash in on the reopening of this major export market. Wilson Boyd on the other hand had, in his own words "huge stocks of whiskey, the up-to-date plant, the goodwill and the trade connection of such an old concern".

Boyd had returned from the States with orders in his back pocket. On 31st November 1933 the first shipment of whiskey left Belfast for New York, in anticipation of the repeal of Prohibition. Wilson Boyd spoke to the *Belfast Telegraph*.

"We are delighted to get the order. The whiskey is to be sent direct to New York and all the necessary licences are in our possession for the shipment. It is the only order, so far as I can find out, to be completed under official permit. We regard it as a great compliment to our firm and it is some recognition of our efforts to secure orders in America. We hope the order is the forerunner of many others."

Indeed it was just the first of a wave of orders to be wired across the Atlantic.

"We have been preparing for America to go wet for more than ten years!" he said at the time.

Boyd's visit to the States had paid off big time, and his vision was richly rewarded. Just twelve days later the *Telegraph* reported that yet another shipment has been ordered.

"It is probably the biggest shipment of bottled whiskey that has ever left an Irish port. The bulk of it is for Chicago."

Within the week the Customs in Belfast port were reported to be working overtime to get the shipment out by Christmas. Boyd had pulled it off: not only had he secured the distillery's future, but in doing so he had captured the vital North American market.

Left: Inside the still house, 1926. On the left next to the spirit safe, note the two fire buckets. One of the riveted wash stills on the right has a flat top accommodating the drive shaft for a rummager, preventing solids in the wash from sticking to the bottom of the still.

THE Strange Fascination
OF THE Seventh DRINK
(NOT, OF COURSE, AT ONE SITTING)
OF BUSHMILLS

● After the seventh drink of Bushmills, men tell us it's the *one* whiskey they would take with them "on a desert island". At first acquaintance, it tastes surprisingly unique. And its strangely fascinating flavor "grows" on you to an irresistible degree. That's why — for 152 years — Bushmills has been the whiskey of connoisseurs! Bushmills appeals to the cultivated taste because it is maltier — and every drop is 9 years old! You'll find that no other whiskey can match the sustained, thrilling flavor of a highball, Manhattan or Old Fashioned made with Bushmills!

The Whiskey that has Everything

ROBUST AS OLD RYE
MELLOW AS OLD BOURBON
TANGY AS OLD SCOTCH

90° PROOF

SHAW — ALEX D. SHAW, IMPORT DIVISION, NATIONAL DISTILLERS PRODUCTS CORP., NEW YORK

AFTER THE SEVENTH DRINK
(NOT, OF COURSE, AT ONE SITTING)
YOU'LL DISCOVER THE REAL APPEAL OF BUSHMILLS!

● We say "after the seventh drink"— because at first acquaintance you might not fully appreciate Bushmills' unique flavor. For, Bushmills is maltier — and 9 years old! Its distinctive taste "grows" on you to an irresistible degree. After the seventh drink — you too will regard Bushmills as the whiskey to be preferred above all others!

Robust as Old Rye
Mellow as Old Bourbon
Tangy as Old Scotch

BUSHMILLS
THE WHISKEY THAT HAS EVERYTHING

90° PROOF

SHAW — NATIONAL DISTILLERS PRODUCTS CORP., SHAW IMPORT DIVISION, N.Y.

---

90 | BUSHMILLS

Left and above: American advertisements from the 1930s. After the War, Bushmills flourished in the US market.

FOUR HUNDRED YEARS IN THE MAKING

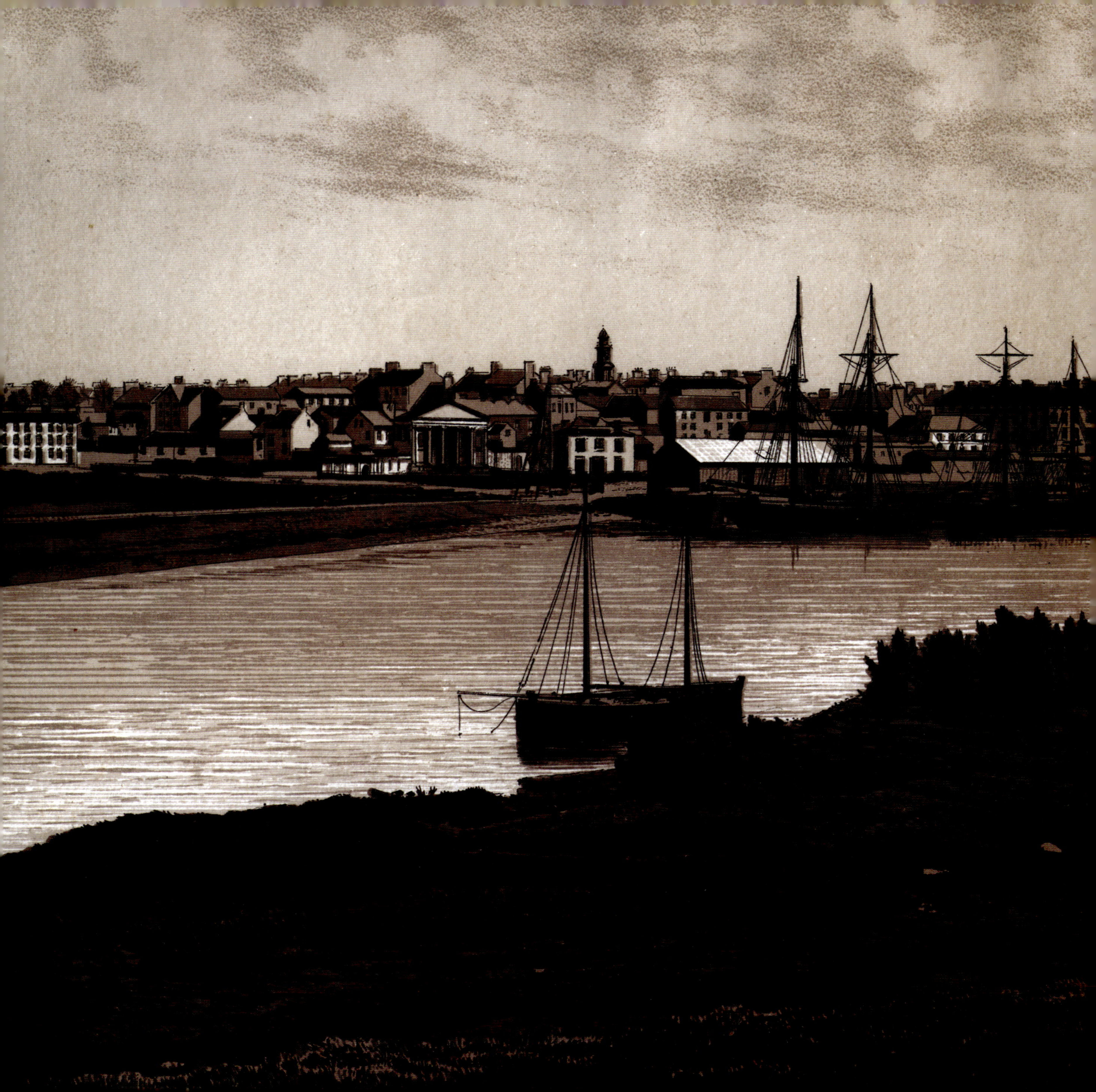

Chapter Twenty

Coleraine

Coleraine is one of the most fondly remembered of Ireland's numerous silent distilleries. The reasons are many: it made good whiskey; it closed relatively recently; and the odd bottle of single malt from 1959 can still be bought, if you have enough money. The 'Coleraine' label has also lived on as a blend; it has a small but loyal following and is sold almost exclusively in Northern Ireland.

Coleraine started life in the mid-1820s and by 1837 its owner, Thomas Black, was advertising "a large supply on sale at his stores, which will be sold cheap for Cash or good Bills". After that nifty line in sales and marketing, it is not surprising that the following year Black sold out to Michael Ferrar.

Ferrar built the company's reputation and by 1845 he was supplying Coleraine Whiskey to the House of Commons in London. Thereafter the initials 'HC' appeared on each and every bottle of Coleraine, as did the crest of the City of London.

Robert Taylor took over the distillery in 1869, and his name hung over the door until the very end. His attention to detail meant this tiny distillery, which never produced more than 100,000 gallons a year, had a fine reputation. In fact after visiting each and every distillery in the then-United Kingdom of Great Britain and Ireland, Alfred Barnard was forced to concede: "In all our wanderings through Erin's Green Isle, for cleanliness, order and regularity, we have seen no distillery to beat this."

Taylor was a clever businessman and a whiskey innovator; this meant that Coleraine was always leading change. When everyone was selling casks to the bonded trade, Taylor installed a bottling plant in the distillery, and while cheap patent blends were flooding the market, Taylor was moving up market, producing a ten-year-old bottling of his own malt whiskey.

After Robert Taylor's death, quality slipped and like every other Irish distillery, Coleraine suffered from the combined

Left: Illustration of Coleraine during the 19th century

Left: Advertisement for Coleraine Whiskey

troubles of the Great War, American Prohibition and political unrest in Ireland. Like so many others concerns, the distillery was mothballed in the early 1920s. Although purchased by William Boyd in 1933 for its stocks of highly regarded whiskey, the plant didn't start back into production until 1938.

If James Watt Morrison was underwhelmed by what he saw when he started work at Old Bushmills, it will come as no surprise to hear he was even less happy with what he found at Coleraine. The boiler had been condemned, the heating tanks in the mash house were rotten through, but more interesting still was the stillroom. It contained four stills and two of them were not even designed to make whiskey. They were brandy stills.

"I had seen photographs of them," recalled Morrison. "They were spheres or balls with the bottom half set in a cast iron casing. They were small with a working content of 150 gallons and an exceedingly long or high head."

Today one of these stills can be seen in the visitors area at the Old Bushmills distillery, but at the time there was no money to change them. The stills had been making good whiskey, so they were pressed into service. Being so small in comparison with the wash stills, they had to be constantly filled and emptied.

A 1938 information sheet gave details of the revived distillery:

"Six months' intensive reconstruction work at the (Coleraine) Distillery culminate at the beginning of this week in the recommencement of the process of distillation. At the present moment whiskey is running from the stills which have been unemployed for a decade and a half, and is well up to the standard of former years."

But Coleraine wasn't long back in business before the Second World War took its toll. Barley was rationed, so the plant was once again mothballed. After the war, when small amounts of barley were released for distilling, Coleraine's quota was used at Old Bushmills. Coleraine hobbled along, but it produced malt whiskey very infrequently. It began to be used more and more as a support facility for Bushmills. The bottling line was moved there, then in 1954 a continuous still was installed in Coleraine; this was the beginning of what would one day become Black Bush whiskey.

Malt whiskey was only distilled periodically here until it ceased altogether in 1964. The bottling hall in Coleraine closed in 1968, and the facility finally fell silent in 1978 when Irish Distillers were in charge. They shifted all the production of grain whiskey to Cork.

During the 1930s right across the island of Ireland the whiskey business was in freefall, so when the tiny Killowen distillery, also in Coleraine, was put up for sale, it was an obvious purchase for Boyd. Killowen never had the kind of reputation that Coleraine enjoyed, but Boyd needed extra warehousing. Killowen was drafted into service to store the output of Bushmills and Coleraine.

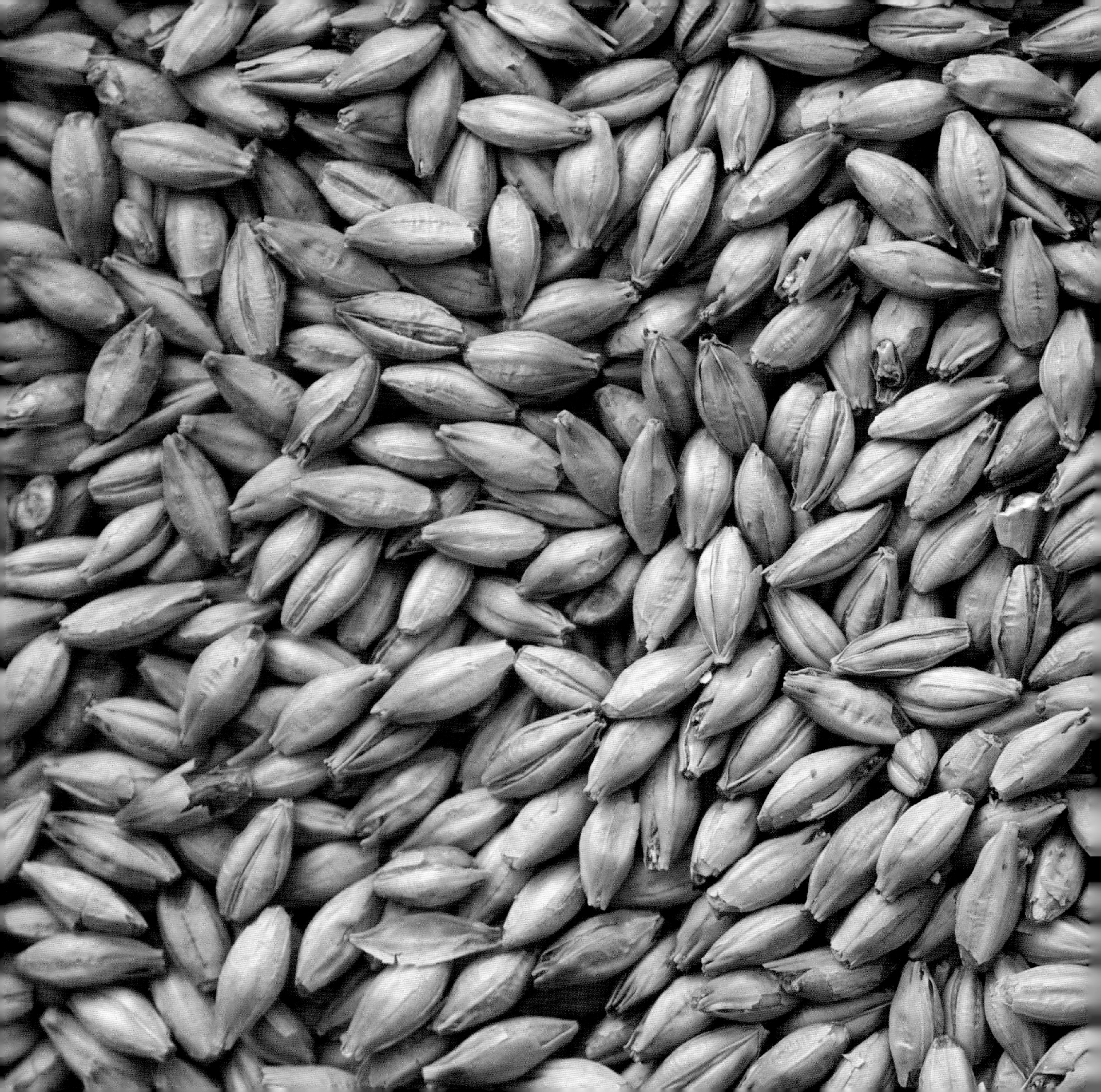

Chapter Twenty One
Of Bushmills and Barley

The Nugent family have had a long association with the whiskey business in Northern Ireland. James Nugent was Managing Director of McConnell's, a Belfast firm of brewers and whiskey bonders. While running the family brewery, his son Chester Nugent started malting barley on contract for Guinness of Dublin in the 1920s. After their own brewery went into liquidation, Chester struck up a relationship with Old Bushmills.

As early as 1932 we know from James Morrison's journal that Old Bushmills was supplying the Dublin brewer:

"…throughout the season I can recall nothing of any real interest to write about, except that on completing our own malting we became Maltsters making on contract through a Belfast businessman, Chester Nugent, malt for Guinness in Dublin."

This early connection between Bushmills and Guinness, two of Ireland's most famous brands, has not been given the attention it deserves. Here were two major drinks companies, who found themselves on different sides of a border, cordially doing business throughout the 1930s and 1940s, at a time when relations between north and south were strained. The Irish Free State dropped the oath of allegiance to the British Crown, declared itself a Republic and remained neutral during the Second World War.

This north-south relationship continued when Chester Nugent and his son Granville opened a new malt house, just outside Belfast. A letter dated 25th April 1941 from the Ards Malting Company to Guinness in Dublin, outlines the problems Nugent was having getting an export licence to send malt south of the border during the war. Chester Nugent writes of the Blitz and "the terrible hammering that we got here last Tuesday week, our Maltings just escaping". Whether or not he knew about the units of the Dublin fire brigade that had crossed the border to help their counterparts in Belfast is not known. Either way he was only able to promise 1,000 barrels of the 8,500 ordered.

Left: Corns of barley. Barley is an essential ingredient in the creation of both whiskey and beer.

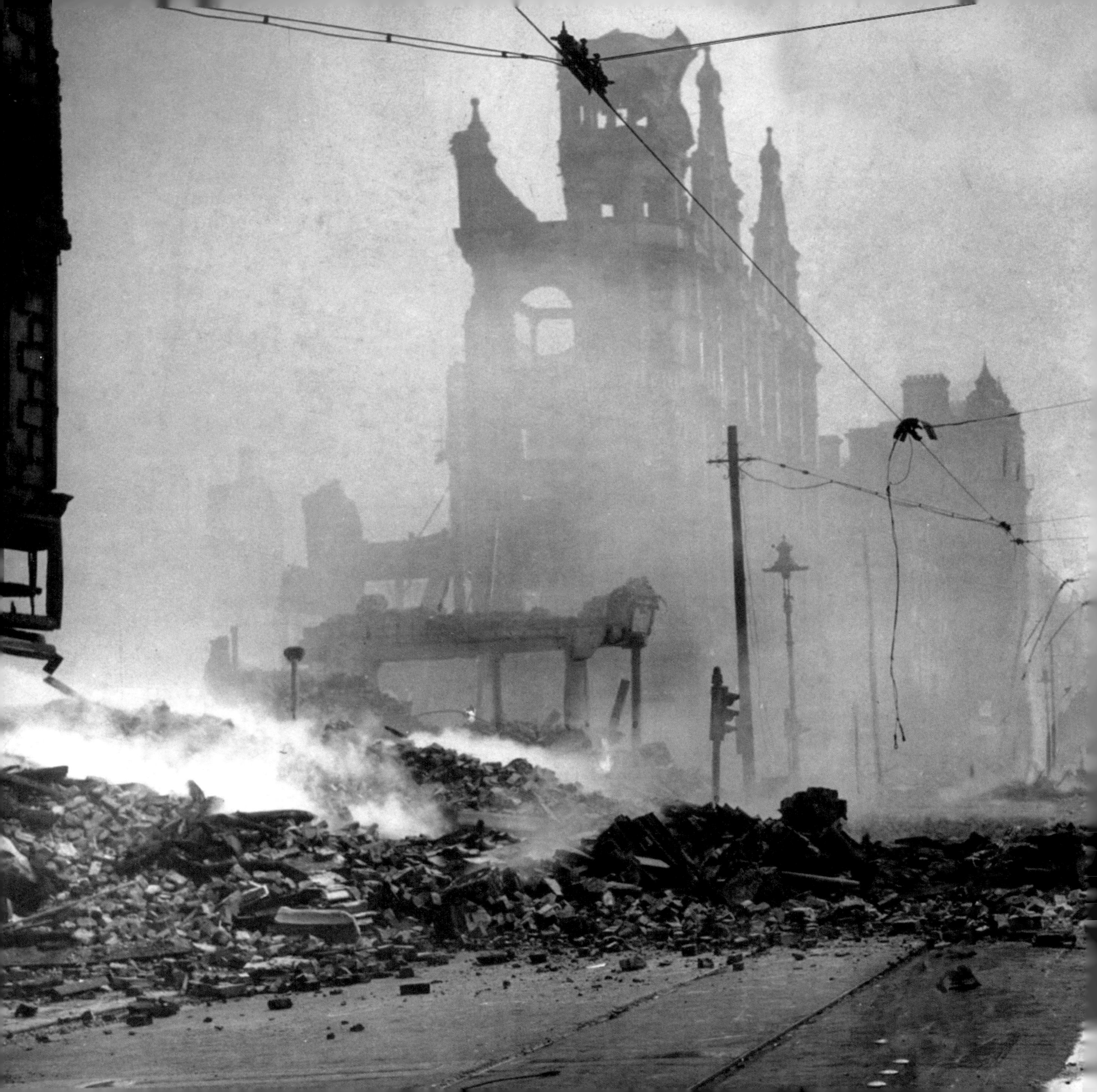

It was clear that supplying Dublin with malt from this own facility was going to be an ongoing problem, but he had a plan. Nugent would try to get the Boyds to handle the brewers' barley.

"I am endeavouring to arrange to malt this at Killowen or Bushmills Maltings, but I do not know whether I will be able to accomplish it or not. These Maltings are at present filled up with Whiskies removed from Belfast by order of the Ministry of Public Security since the last 'blitz'."

The Luftwaffe raid on Belfast had been deadly. Vast parts of the city had been levelled: the Boyds had lost their Hill Street headquarters. Not only were valuable papers gone, but a bonded warehouse full of precious and rare mature whiskey went up in smoke. The resulting fire raged so fiercely that steel beams buckled and the building smouldered for a week. After this all remaining whiskey was moved out of Belfast.

It is clear that Guinness badly needed malt supplies from Northern Ireland:

"We would emphasise that we really require as much as possible, and are willing to pay for it."

It is also clear Nugent was doing his best to supply them:

"At the moment we are negotiating for the Maltings at Bushmills Distillery, in the hope that we may be able to malt there next season."

Both sides kept in constant contact during this difficult period, and from the letters that crossed between Belfast to Dublin, we can get a really good picture of what was happening in all three of the Boyd distilleries during the war.

Left: The aftermath of a raid during the Belfast Blitz. Through the smoke and dust we can see the forlorn figure of the Albert Clock in the background.

FOUR HUNDRED YEARS IN THE MAKING

In July, Nugent wrote:

"Killowen, although not altered very much, is still occupied by the Military…Bushmills is a rather different proposition, as the bottom floor of the Malt House is now a Bond Store and full of Whiskey to the utmost at the moment. Windows have all been built up and a wall built across it to conform to British Customs regulations which you know are very very strict…There is another old Malting at Comber Distillery which I will inspect shortly, but I hardly think it is suitable."

The inspection Nugent speaks of was published in August 1941 and his *Report on Malting Accommodation in Northern Ireland* catches the industry at the very point of death. Five of the six Maltings Nugent visited had been attached to breweries or distilleries, and a generation earlier they had been working to full capacity. What Nugent found made very sobering reading.

The Old McConnell's Brewery had, he wrote "been altered so much that they could not be used for Malting purposes or drying grain." The silent Dunville's Distillery was found to be "full of wood stored there on behalf of the Northern Ireland Government…The kiln attached to this building is dismantled." Then there was what remained of Northern Ireland's recent distilling industry. Old Comber was found to be "completely unsuitable…there is no machinery of any description". Killowen was "occupied by the Military, housing 100 soldiers. The two barley lofts are used as sleeping quarters…the malting floor has been divided across from wall to wall by two brick divisions, one part used as a cook-house, the other as a canteen". Even if these walls were ripped out, Killowen's potential capacity was tiny, estimated at 50 tons per week.

Then there was Old Bushmills, which "could be used for Malting purposes if the Whiskey now stored in the ground working floor was removed and the brick wall 43 ft long, across the house also removed".

By September Guinness were still waiting to hear if they would get malt from Bushmills. Chester wrote to Wilson Boyd on the 16th of the month asking:

"When do you think you would be in a position to come to any definite decision?"

Wilson Boyd was playing a waiting game. He was trying to get a licence to distil and if successful, there wouldn't be enough time in the season to both supply Guinness and distil whiskey. It was another two years before Guinness got the good news they had been waiting for. On 23rd August 1943 Chester Nugent confirmed in a letter to the brewer:

"I have been able to get the use of the Bushmills Malt House and provided no unforeseen circumstance would arise, such as occupation by the Military or interference by the British Customs and Excise, I think I would be able to do it."

By the end of the Second World War, a tradition that had started some twenty years earlier recommenced, as Old Bushmills started malting again for Guinness of Dublin. But it was not to continue; the days of the distillery producing its own malt were numbered. The future lay in the sixth and final malt house, of which Nugent wrote – his own Ards Malt Company. This was a state-of-the-art complex "in first class repair. Being a new Maltings, it is up-to-date in every way and capable of drying 140 tons of grain per week."

If the Bushmills maltings couldn't cut it, it was also clear that there was no future for Killowen. There is however one final story about Killowen. During the war it was used to store the casks of maturing Bushmills that had been taken out of Belfast. It was also used as a base for US soldiers. It is not surprising that Jimmy Morrison's suspicions were aroused when, despite having the necessary paperwork, he was refused access to the Killowen site. He returned with the local police chief to find American troops had been helping themselves to the maturing whiskey. The 'free bar' was closed and within 48 hours all the American troops had been moved somewhere less exciting.

By the end of the Second World War the price of whiskey had increased from 10 shillings a proof gallon to more than 200 shillings. By 1945 the maturing whiskey stocks that had been laid down since the mid-1930s were now approaching their tenth birthday. The Boyd family, who had invested heavily in whiskey since the early 1930s, were sitting on liquid gold. They were also facing a windfall tax, with no easy get-out clause like after the First World War. That loophole had been closed in 1938. With the growth of global branding, the days of the family-run distillery were numbered.

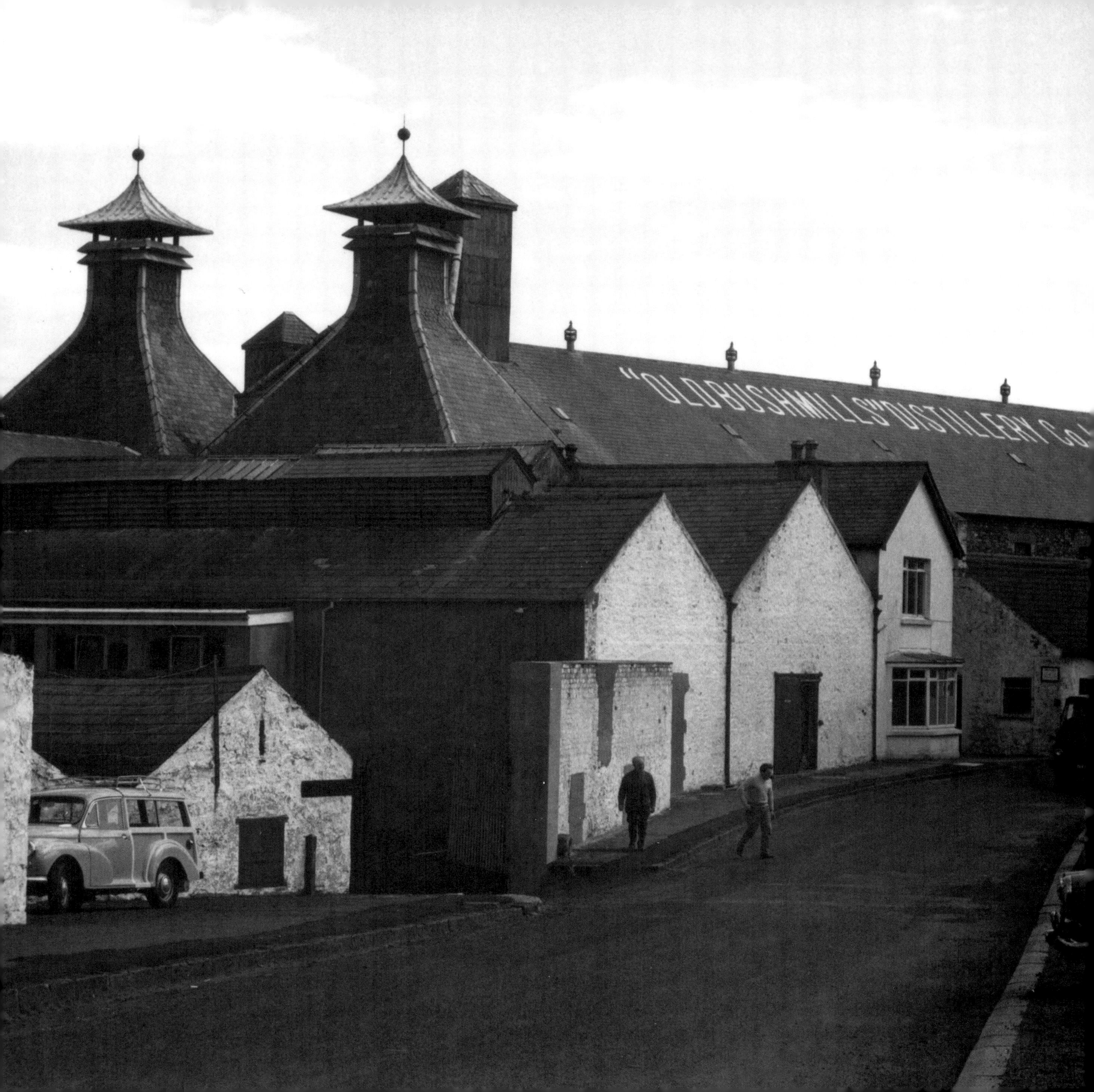
"OLD BUSHMILLS" DISTILLERY Co

Chapter Twenty Two

Big Business

In December 1962, the year he was awarded a knighthood, *Time* magazine ran a profile of the boss of Great Universal Stores, the sixty-five-year-old Sir Isaac Wolfson:

"Sir Isaac himself is a teetotaler and nonsmoker, who proudly insists that his personal expenses are covered by a shilling (14¢) a day. 'The Gov'nor', as employees call him, still arrives at his red-carpeted office every morning at 7.45 a.m., works through till 5 or 6 p.m."

Nowadays GUS plc has two separate divisions, one includes Argos, the UK's largest catalogue retailer, the other is the Experian credit reporting agency. When Glasgow-born Wolfson joined GUS in 1932, *Time* magazine reported that the company "was a consistent money loser…Gussie's shares, now worth 450 times what they were when Sir Isaac joined the company."

Knowing how to make friends and influence people, throughout the war Wolfson had kept the 'hard to get hold of' Bushmills on hand to impress his guests. So he must have been surprised when, shortly after the war, he found himself face to face with Wilson Boyd at a business lunch in Belfast. Legend has it that Wolfson came right out and asked if Boyd was willing to sell the distillery as a going concern. Boyd's answer isn't recorded, but almost immediately Wolfson started buying into the distillery. Although the Boyd Brothers stayed on as company directors, by 1946 GUS had acquired a controlling interest in both Old Bushmills and Coleraine distilleries.

Before his acquisition of Old Bushmills, Wolfson wasn't in the drinks trade, but he was very much in the business of buying, selling and making money. GUS had deep pockets, and although life in the distillery went on as it ever had, the future of Old Bushmills was being secured.

In the book *Spirit of the Age: Story of Old Bushmills*, the company chartered accountant Rollo McClure remembers the distillery at this period.

Left: The distillery in the late 1960s.

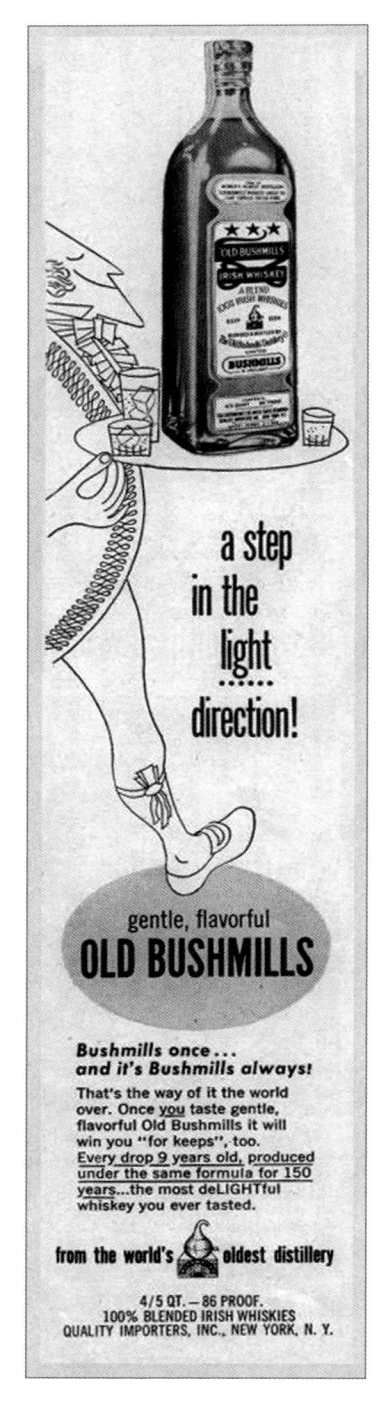

PIONEER'S TALE!

The thousands upon thousands who discovered Old Bushmills Irish Coffee (initiating one of the profound love affairs of recent years)—began recognizing that the irresistible flavor-characteristic was a delight *in-and-for itself*.. a great whiskey with an easy, lovely flavor.. a triumph of Irish taste.. the gay, unique and taste-satisfying genius of one of the world's great whiskeys.

We offer *you* the secret of consummate whiskey—Old Bushmills' lovely flavor —in the many ways the recent discoverers in the New World are enjoying it—*On-the-Rocks, Highball, Irish Coffee, Bushmills 'n Bitters*. Whichever way you begin this experience in discernibly greater enjoyment, you will find the necessary ingredient, grand Old Bushmills, anywhere in the world.

OLD BUSHMILLS
Irish Whiskey
IMPORTED FROM THE WORLD'S OLDEST DISTILLERY
86 PROOF. 100% BLENDED IRISH WHISKIES. QUALITY IMPORTERS, INC., NEW YORK, N.Y.

1st—SUPERB WHISKEY
OLD BUSHMILLS

2nd—FOR ALL PURPOSES
OLD BUSHMILLS

3rd—WITH LOVELY FLAVOUR
OLD BUSHMILLS

4th—FOR SUPERIOR TASTES
OLD BUSHMILLS

FOR A DELIGHTFUL CHANGE
AND A LASTING ONE—

OLD BUSHMILLS
the classic
IRISH WHISKEY

86 PROOF. 100% BLENDED IRISH WHISKIES. QUALITY IMPORTERS, INC., NEW YORK, N.Y.

---

a step in the light direction!

gentle, flavorful
OLD BUSHMILLS

Bushmills once... and it's Bushmills always! That's the way of it the world over. Once *you* taste gentle, flavorful Old Bushmills it will win you "for keeps", too. Every drop 9 years old, produced under the same formula for 150 years...the most deLIGHTful whiskey you ever tasted.

from the world's oldest distillery

4/5 QT. — 86 PROOF.
100% BLENDED IRISH WHISKIES
QUALITY IMPORTERS, INC., NEW YORK, N.Y.

---

104 | BUSHMILLS

Above: 1950s advertising for the American market

"[It was] a good solid business, though the turnover was not all that great. In the early days the sales were confined to Ireland and exports went mostly to England and North America. But under Wolfson they began to export all over the world. I was required to make a monthly analysis and exports were sent to practically anywhere you could name."

Up until this point the vast majority of the small Irish distilleries relied very heavily on local sales. Thanks to Wilson Boyd, Old Bushmills was available in foreign markets, but in reality the amounts were relatively small. By pushing Old Bushmills around the world, Wolfson was expanding its fan base, securing foreign markets and thereby cushioning the distillery from any more major shocks to the already shaky domestic market.

Throughout the 1950s and 1960s sales to the United States increased rapidly. The reputation of Old Bushmills grew and grew, thanks in no small part to Col. Henry Kaplan of Quality Importers. Kaplan was an energetic and incredibly focused businessman, who had served in the army (he retained his military title) and made fortunes many times over in various drink-based industries. He was a close personal friend of Isaac Wolfson, and after the Second World War Kaplan set up Quality Importers. He put his not inconsiderable energies into marketing Ambassador De Luxe Scotch and later Bushmills.

He was a brand ambassador *extraordinaire*. For thirty years he lived in a suite at the Waldorf Hotel and courted film stars, journalists, horse trainers – anyone who could help him sell his whiskey. One of his favourite haunts was the '21' club on New York's West 52nd St. In Capote's novella *Breakfast at Tiffany's* this is where the narrator first spots Holly Golightly.

In *The Spirit of the Age* Kaplan's long time associate Sol Aleles recalls a story which just about sums him up.

"He took it as a personal affront if any of his close friends ordered anything other than Ambasador De Luxe or Old Bushmills…Henry was the greatest salesman I ever knew. One day we were flying from the West Coast to New York but Henry announced suddenly, 'I'm stopping off at Omaha.' I asked in surprise, 'Whatever for?' and Henry said 'I don't think they are doing enough in Nebraska.' So we took yet another flight to Omaha, and we checked in at a local hotel. Henry asked them to give him flashlamps, and we went around the town in the darkness shining the lamps into the windows of liquor stores to check if Ambassador and Old Bushmills were on display. In no time at all the police picked us up and asked what the hell we were doing. We had to talk our way out of that one, but that's the kind of salesman Henry was!"

Kaplan and Wolfson's efforts were paying off. By the early 1970s Bushmills had become the largest selling Irish whiskey in the United States. But their success at this time should be kept in perspective. Back in the 1950s 'whiskey' meant 'Scotch', and that meant blended whiskey. Scotch then and not Irish was the drink of choice on Madison Avenue. Ireland simply didn't have the brands, the expertise or the muscle to crack the American market. In 1955, only 140,458 gallons of whiskey in total were exported from the Republic of Ireland, up a paltry 12,683 gallons in twenty years. There wasn't a distillery on the island, north or south, whose whiskies were getting the kinds of sales enjoyed by Johnnie Walker or J&B. Irish distilleries were very small players in what was becoming a global industry, dominated by multi-nationals.

93
WHAT'S SO IRISH ABOUT THIS FOURSOME?
THE OLD BUSHMILLS IN EVERY DRINK!
On-the-Rocks, in a Sour, an Old Fashioned or in the latest delight, Irish Coffee, the smoothness of OLD BUSHMILLS makes any drink "Click". It's that exceptional liqueur quality that makes the difference. Try it and become a devotee of excellence.
OLD BUSHMILLS
IRISH WHISKEY
PRODUCT OF THE WORLD'S OLDEST DISTILLERY
Try your next MANHATTAN with OLD BUSHMILLS Click!
Try your next OLD FASHIONED with OLD BUSHMILLS Click!
Try your next WHISKEY SOUR with OLD BUSHMILLS Click!
Try your next ON-THE-ROCKS with OLD BUSHMILLS Click!
Try your next STINGER with OLD BUSHMILLS Click!
SEND FOR THESE BEAUTIFUL IRISH COFFEE GLASSES
A SET OF FOUR (4) EXQUISITE GOLD-EMBELLISHED GLASSES (RETAIL VALUE $4) ONLY $2.50, POSTPAID. MAIL CHECK OR MONEY ORDER (NO CASH OR STAMPS, PLEASE!) BUSHMILLS GLASSES, DEPARTMENT A., BOX 1284, GRAND CENTRAL STA., NEW YORK 17, N. Y.
86 PROOF. 100% BLENDED IRISH WHISKIES. QUALITY IMPORTERS, INC., NEW YORK, N. Y.
1961

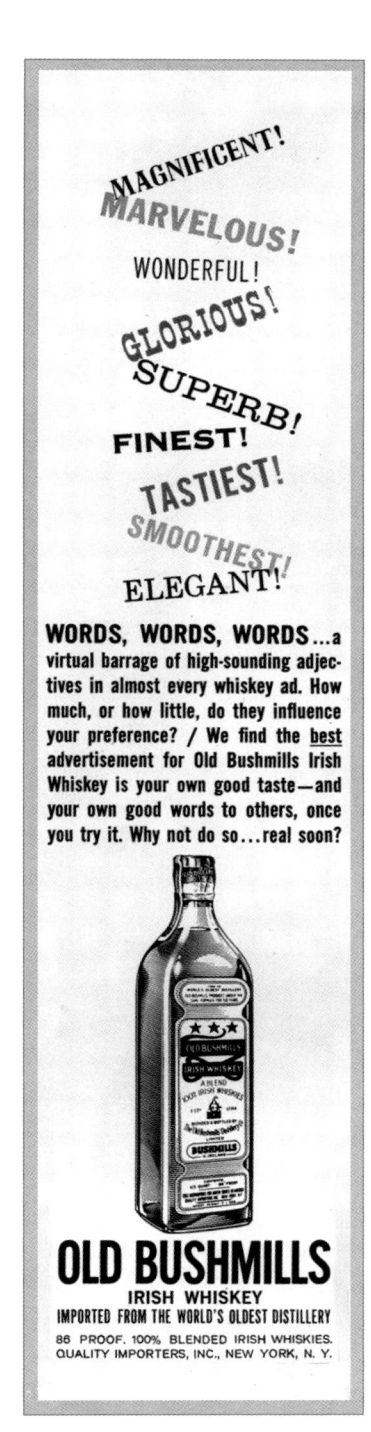

MAGNIFICENT!
MARVELOUS!
WONDERFUL!
GLORIOUS!
SUPERB!
FINEST!
TASTIEST!
SMOOTHEST!
ELEGANT!

WORDS, WORDS, WORDS...a virtual barrage of high-sounding adjectives in almost every whiskey ad. How much, or how little, do they influence your preference? / We find the best advertisement for Old Bushmills Irish Whiskey is your own good taste—and your own good words to others, once you try it. Why not do so...real soon?

OLD BUSHMILLS
IRISH WHISKEY
IMPORTED FROM THE WORLD'S OLDEST DISTILLERY
86 PROOF. 100% BLENDED IRISH WHISKIES.
QUALITY IMPORTERS, INC., NEW YORK, N. Y.

The Whiskey that's made it
STYLISH TO DRINK IRISH

You hear it oftener than ever: "Make it with Old Bushmills". A mighty smart rule to follow, whatever drink you favor. It's that unique liqueur quality—an Old Bushmills' extra—that makes any drink taste enjoyably smoother, tastier. Try it in your favorite!

OLD BUSHMILLS
IRISH WHISKEY
BOTTLED IN IRELAND
at the world's oldest distillery.

86 PROOF / 100% BLENDED IRISH WHISKIES / QUALITY IMPORTERS INC., N.Y.

---

taste it!...

......then write your own ad!

86 PROOF. 100% BLENDED IRISH WHISKIES.
QUALITY IMPORTERS, INC., NEW YORK, N. Y.

Left and Above: 1960s advertising for the American market

FOUR HUNDRED YEARS IN THE MAKING | 107

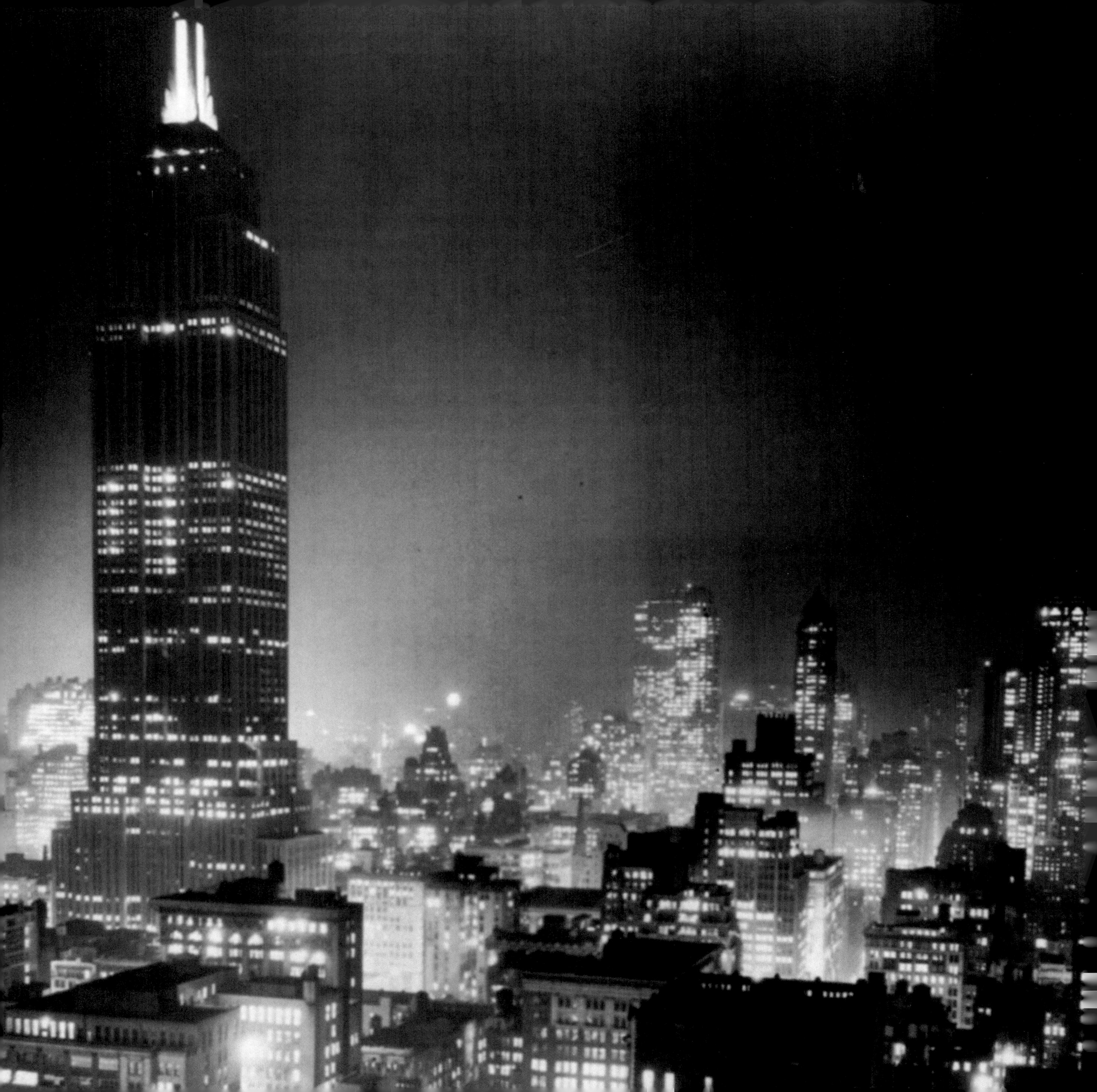

Chapter Twenty Three
New York

On Sunday morning, 24th April 1960, six men got off an Aer Lingus plane at New York's Idlewild airport. One of them was Austin Boyd.

The New York Times reported on their arrival and intentions.

"The visit is frankly and emphatically 'for the sake of the dear sales curve'…The visitors hope that all America will be prepared to rally around their brands – Dunphy's Original Irish, Gilbey's Crock of Gold, John Jameson's, Murphy's, Old Bushmills, Paddy, Powers Gold Label and Tullamore Dew."

Six men representing eight brands, the members of the Irish Whiskey and Distillers Association had arrived in New York with business on their mind. They had rented a townhouse and advertised a drinks party. Not surprisingly they got 30,000 replies, but they had only 600 places: the whole thing was a farce. The event's purpose was never made clear – were they promoting their individual brands, or Irish whiskey as a whole? What would they do with the 20,400 people, all prospective customers they had excluded from the party? And where was the follow up? Simple: there wasn't any. The whole event now typifies the kind of collective folly that gripped the Irish whiskey industry. Rome was on fire, and everyone was in New York fiddling.

By 1965 exports of Irish whiskey were up, but there was nothing to celebrate; and it had nothing to do with that sales trip to New York. Exports were up because the Kilbeggan distillery, which had closed its doors in the early 1950s, finally sold off its huge stocks of mature whiskey. At the time of closing, business had been so bad, there was enough unsold whiskey to maintain their current sales for a hundred years.

By the mid-1960s then there was very little to celebrate, but the pointless New York mission by the Irish Whiskey and Distillers Association had at least shown that all the distilleries

Left: The New York skyline

on the island could cooperate when they needed to. Before too long they would have to do so again, this time to stop themselves from vanishing off the face of the earth altogether.

Chapter Twenty Four
Charrington

With the exception of Old Bushmills, every Irish distillery was still family owned. Although GUS was a large concern, it was not a player in the global drinks industry. By the early 1960s Sir Isaac Wolfson was looking for a way out, and for all the bluster about booming sales, Old Bushmills was selling just 24,000 cases each year in their home market of Northern Ireland.

At the time Charringtons were one of Britain's largest brewers. In 1964 they owned 4,900 tied houses and 655 off-licenses. They were already in the whiskey business, as they owned Auchentoshan distillery near Glasgow; they also operated a brewery in Northern Ireland.

The arrival of Charrington was inevitable. Right across the economy, companies in fields as diverse as banking and brewing were merging and consolidating. Larger firms, with specialist knowledge of specific markets were becoming more and more common, and all the while the world was getting smaller and smaller.

In one form or another Charringtons had been in the beer business since 1738, and it still had a family member at the helm. John Charrington was no stranger to the north Antrim coast, having been stationed there during the Second World War. It is not surprising that it was a personal relationship that put him into contact with Old Bushmills.

In 1961 Charringtons took over the Belfast-based wine and spirit merchants Lyle and Kinahan. John Charrington struck up a friendship with Sir Robin Kinahan. Although the Kinahan family originally came from Co. Cork and Robin's great-great-grandfather had been Lord Mayor of Dublin, he was a Unionist and a prominent member of the Orange Order. But he also deplored bigotry and sectarianism – his Belfast office employed both Protestant and Catholic workers.

Sir Robin knew everybody in the drinks industry in Northern Ireland at that time, and as a director of

Charrington United Breweries, he was well placed to act as matchmaker. With GUS looking for a way out of distilling, and with John Charrington looking for acquisitions, one fine day in the spring of 1964, both men came calling to the sleepy village of Bushmills.

A deal was done and Charrington Kinahan Ltd. took over Old Bushmills for £750,000 cash and a million shares in Charrington United. The plan was a simple one: the parent company owned plenty of bars and off-licenses, and it would quickly be able to get Old Bushmills into more outlets than ever right across Great Britain.

When the news of the take over broke on July 17th 1964 it hit the front page of the *Belfast News Letter*. The secret had been so well kept, that this was the first most of the distillery workers knew about it. It was also the end of another era. Wilson Boyd took this opportunity to retire; he hadn't been well and his brother Austin succeeded him as MD.

Around this time a lot of things changed in the distillery. Until 1964 whiskey making at Old Bushmills was a seasonal job. Distilling would start in the late autumn when the barley had been harvested and malted, and would continue into early summer. With the arrival of Charrington, money was pumped into the distillery and the production season started to expand until it filled the entire year.

It was clear that under GUS there had been underinvestment and unwillingness to take difficult decisions about manning levels, management structure and economies of scale. The changes were soon in coming and when them came, it was clear that the future of Bushmills would be secured at the expense of Coleraine.

The Coleraine bottling hall was to be closed and a new one built on site in Bushmills as part of a £1.25 million expansion. In three short years a maturation warehouse joined the new bottling hall, but perhaps most significant was a new blending area.

Within a year sales to the USA were up by 25%, while UK sales were up 19%. Previous underinvestment came back to bite, when sales of Black Bush outstripped matured stocks of whiskey. It was a sign of a deeper malaise. By the end of the decade Charrington had merged with Bass to become the largest brewer in the UK. The company now commanded over 18% of the domestic market: now, more than ever, the company was focused on beer.

While there are many similarities between beer and the whiskey business, there is one significant difference. Beer doesn't have to be matured; brewers can therefore respond very quickly to changing consumer demand. Whiskey makers are forever planning not a month, or a year, but a decade or more ahead.

Consumer demand was also changing. White spirits were becoming more and more popular, particularly with women. Vodka doesn't require maturation, and was proving a very lucrative sideline for the brewers who had a vodka label. In the early days of the vodka revolution more than 95% of the UK market was supplied by British-made vodka, with a third of that market taken by vodka labels owned by brewers, like Charringtons 'Imperial'.

The rise in white spirits coincided with a slide in sales of whiskey and other brown spirits. The whiskey market had also started to fragment, as the public grew more sophisticated and moved away from generic drinks. In other words, instead of asking for a 'gin and tonic' or a 'whiskey and soda' in their local, people were looking for the kind of brands that were advertised on television or in magazines.

The British Monopolies Commission published a report into the drinks industry in April 1969:

"non-brewery owned distillers hold the major share of the United Kingdom market with a small number of brands [like]... Haig, Johnnie Walker, White Horse, Black and White, Dewar's and VAT 69 whiskies."

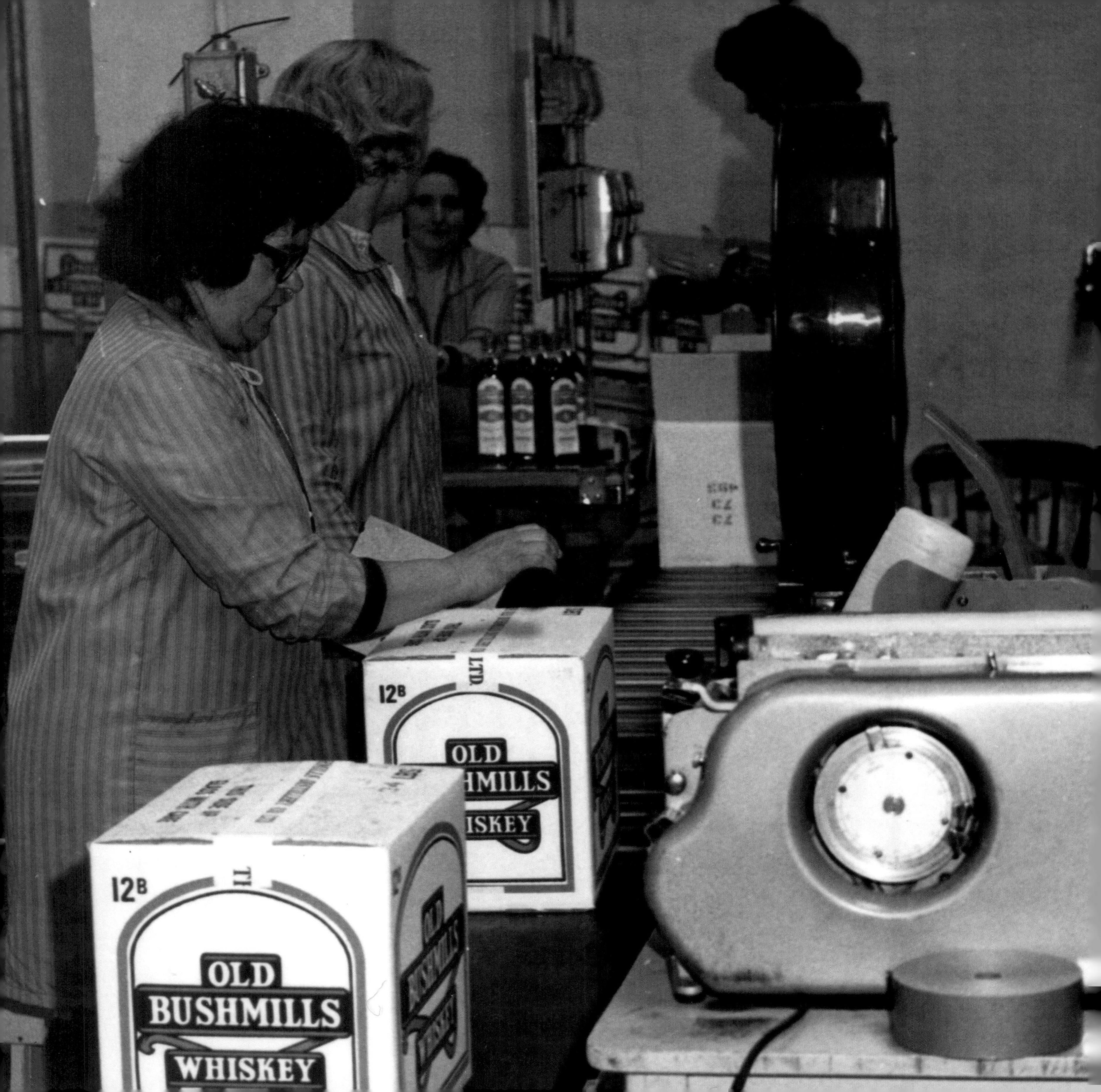
12B
LTD.
OLD
12B
OLD
BUSHMILLS
WHISKEY

in a green field site behind the old Midleton Distillery in Co. Cork, then one by one the last three Victorian plants were closed. On a Friday night in September 1975 the stills finally fell cold in the Old Midleton distillery. There were now just two distilleries on the island, the newest one in Cork and the oldest, Bushmills on the North Antrim coast.

The Irish have a great way of understating things, in the neutral Republic of Ireland, the Second World War was called 'The Emergency', likewise the violence that ripped through the province of Ulster from the late 1960s to the late 1990s is simply referred to as 'The Troubles'.

It was a difficult time to do business in Northern Ireland and things weren't helped by the economic situation. By 1971 the UK was slipping into recession: inflation had risen to 9.4%; Charringtons were trying to sell a distillery and almost no one seemed interested in buying.

"Bushmills was the only distillery in Ireland that was not part of Irish Distillers," recalls Richard Burrows, former Managing Director of Irish Distillers. "The logic was that we acquire it. But there was no movement." Exactly why there was "no movement" on Irish Distillers' offer for Old Bushmills still isn't clear, but both distilleries were about to be overtaken by events when Sam Bronfman picked up the phone.

In the early 1970s Seagram was the largest distilling company in the world. They owned 36 distilleries and '7 Crown', the biggest selling US whiskey. Based in Canada, it was well prepared for the end of Prohibition in the United States and had made a fortune. The man behind

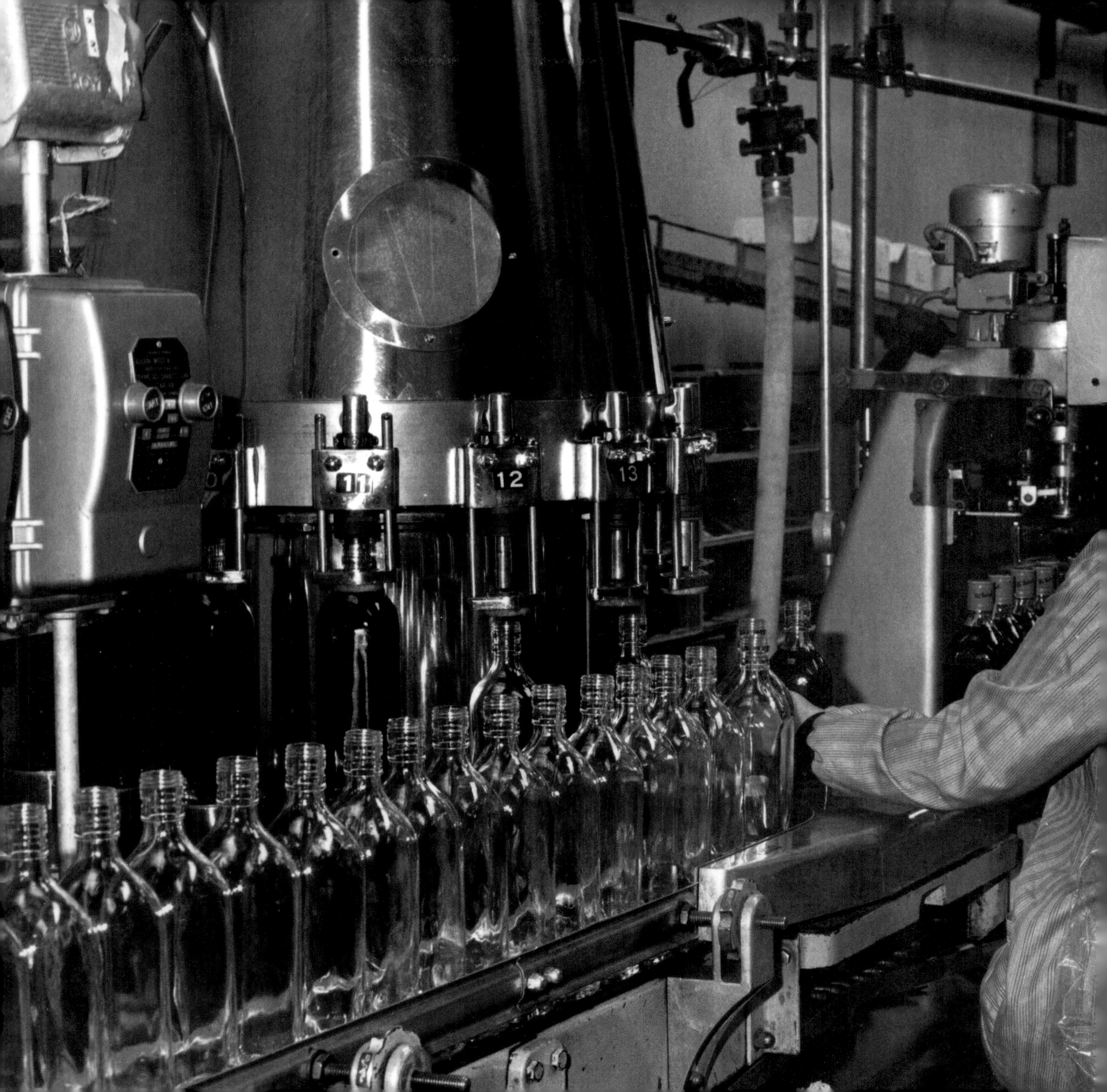
11
12
13

Chapter Twenty Five
Irish Distillers Group

By the mid-1960s there was effectively just one working distillery left in Northern Ireland. In the Republic only three remained; John Jameson and John Power in Dublin and the Cork Distilleries Company – the stump of a once great industry.

The domestic market was contracting and exports were flat. The vast Victorian distilleries were expensive to operate and grossly inefficient. There was a huge duplication of resources and no one had enough money left to turn an Irish whiskey into a global brand.

With Old Bushmills then a part of the Charrington empire, John Clement Ryan, the last member of the Power family to work in the Dublin distillery, saw only one way forward: merger!

On 8th March 1966 John Power & Son, John Jameson & Son and the Cork Distilling Company put centuries of rivalry behind them and amalgamated to form the Irish Distillers Group (IDG).

For two years, for fear of offending any of the founding families, IDG survived without a Managing Director. Then in 1968 in a break with tradition, an outsider was appointed to the post. Kevin McCourt had just finished a five-year contract as Director General of the newly launched Irish TV service, RTÉ. He clearly learnt from the mistakes of the Dublin Whiskey Distillers (DWD) which had floundered in the early decades of the century. To survive, the Irish Distillers Group could not operate as an alliance of three separate companies. They would have to totally reinvent themselves.

"It was tragic but inescapable," remembers John Clement Ryan. "Kevin had to persuade the Board to close all the existing distilleries and replace them with one modern one. It was a huge gamble, but it had to be done."

Irish Distillers also stopped the centuries old practice of selling their whiskey to merchants and started selling direct to the public. A brand new plant costing £9 million was built

Above: US advertising, 1968. By the late 1960s Old Bushmills had become a tasty takeover target.

In other words the move was away from manufacturing to marketing, from making whiskey to packaging and selling it. By the late 1960s Bass-Charrington was adapting to keep ahead of the market. It sold Auchentoshan, the only distillery in Scotland to practice triple distillation. The company then purchased an agency for one of the brands that was being asked for in British pubs and off-licenses – VAT 69. By the early 1970s it was only a matter of time before Bass-Charrington would offload Old Bushmills.

Left: In the cooperage, late 1960s. Davy Gault, then an apprentice cooper, helps cooper John Hanna mend a Sherry butt. Today, Davy is a lorry driver and the longest-serving employee at the distillery...and a star of Bushmills' "Irish at its Best" advertising campaign, shot on site in 2007 (see p. 174).

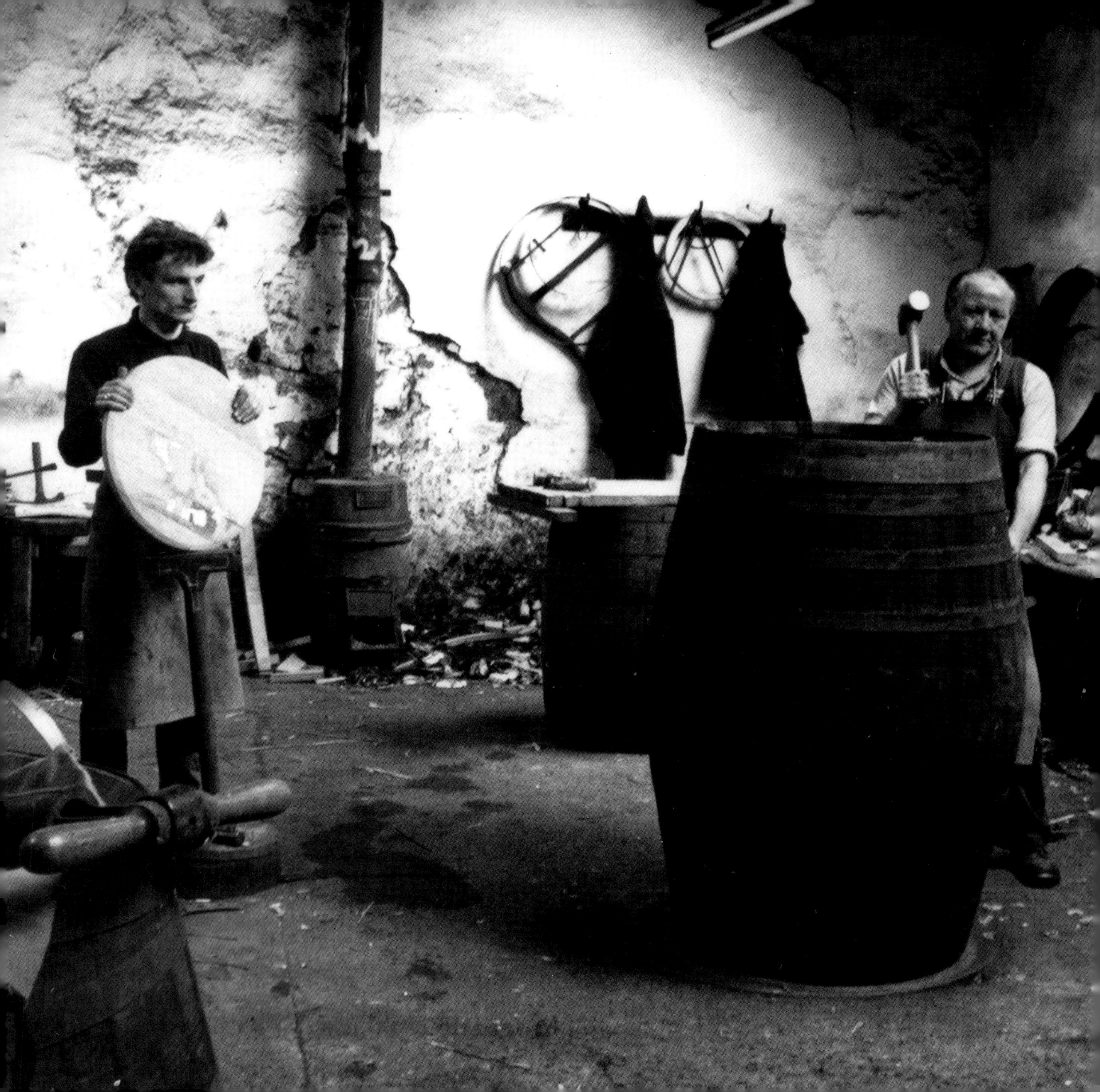

IRELAND
12 FIFTHS
COPY OF ORIGINAL GRANT MADE IN 1608 TO DISTIL WHISKEY
OLD BUSHMILLS
OLD BUSHMILLS
12 FIFTHS
PRODUCED UNDER THE SAME FORMULA
FOR 150 YEARS
AT THE WORLD'S OLDEST DISTILLERY
OLD BUSHMILLS
IRISH WHISKEY
DISTILLED AND BOTTLED IN
IRELAND
OLD BUSHMILLS DISTILLERY CO., LTD.
421
417
413
397
393
389

the company was Sam Bronfman. As John Clement Ryan put it, "he wanted the 'tiny minnow' of Irish Distillers." While the Seagram offer was a friendly one, it was clear to all at Irish Distillers that it was only a matter of time before there would be another approach. The next one might not be so friendly.

"The situation was delicate and Kevin McCourt (Managing Director of Irish Distillers) played it beautifully," says John Clement Ryan, whose father Clem Ryan went on to sit on the Board of Old Bushmills. McCourt offered Seagram a chunk of Irish Distillers, and in return he wanted Bronfman to deliver the previously unobtainable Old Bushmills. This offer must have appealed to Seagram, as they would now have a stake in every glass of whiskey that came from Ireland.

On Friday 13th October 1972, when the news broke that Seagram had bought the Old Bushmills Distillery for £4 million cash, no one could have suspected what was going on behind the scenes. By the following Wednesday *The Irish Times* was reporting that the Seagram had bought Irish Distillers, adding that an international partner was long overdue and that "since Irish Distillers was formed it has had an unexciting record".

Things were not as simple as they first appeared. Seagram were not taking over Irish Distillers; they simply bought a 15% stake in the company for £3.35 million, while at the same time selling Irish Distillers 25% of Old Bushmills, for £1 million cash.

Not only had McCourt secured the Co. Antrim distillery, but he had £2.35 million in the bank. With the Canadians owning part of Irish Distillers, they were, for the moment anyway, immune from any other take-over bid.

With the acquisition of Bushmills, Irish Distillers now controlled the only three working distilleries on the island – Midleton, Bushmills and Coleraine. Irish Distillers was the Irish whiskey industry, and on 10th May 1972, they bought another 55% of Old Bushmills for £2,267,000. (It would be January 1978 before Irish Distillers secured the final 20% of Old Bushmills.)

Initially Irish Distillers invested heavily in Bushmills. They ordered three new stills and almost doubled output. Richard Burrows, was sent north to work on the project.

"The place needed a lot of money spent," he recalled. "It had charm and style, but a lot needed doing."

To this day Burrows is still spoken of fondly around the distillery. He still arrives unannounced, and when he does he doesn't want to talk to the suits; he hunts down the guys he worked with for a good chat.

With their acquisition of Old Bushmills, Irish Distillers now had larger economies of scale; but they also had a very large plant in Midleton. The grain whiskey from Coleraine was no longer needed, and in 1978 its column stills fell cold. From then on Midleton would supply all the group's grain whiskey needs. This also changed the nature of the whiskey coming from Bushmills.

"I look for sweetness, mellowness and overtones of peat," said Austin Boyd when talking about the kind of whiskey made at Bushmills. But following the take-over, in line with every other Irish whiskey, Bushmills would be un-peated. The Bushmills Maltings then were closed, with the requirement for un-peated malt contracted out.

There were now just two distilleries on the island. Midleton and Old Bushmills between them produced fifteen whiskeys, four vodkas, two gins and a rum. It had been one hell of a ride; in less than a century Irish whiskey had gone from global domination, to almost total annihilation.

In 1975 vodka became the biggest selling drink in the States, and in the same year American sales of Irish whiskey were so small (.006%), they weren't even published in *Business Week*'s review of the spirit sales. In global terms, the

OLD BUSHMILLS DISTILLERY C
LICENSED DISTILLERS · ESTed I

newly expanded Irish Distillers was still a tiny concern and 50% of group sales were in the Republic of Ireland. The future then was far from certain, but at least there *was* a future.

The one thing that is certain about the drinks industry is that nothing remains the same for long. By the late 1980s Seagram wanted to off-load their investment in Irish Distillers. The stage was set for the biggest take-over battle in Irish history.

124 | BUSHMILLS

Above: US advertising from 1972

Above: US advertising from 1981

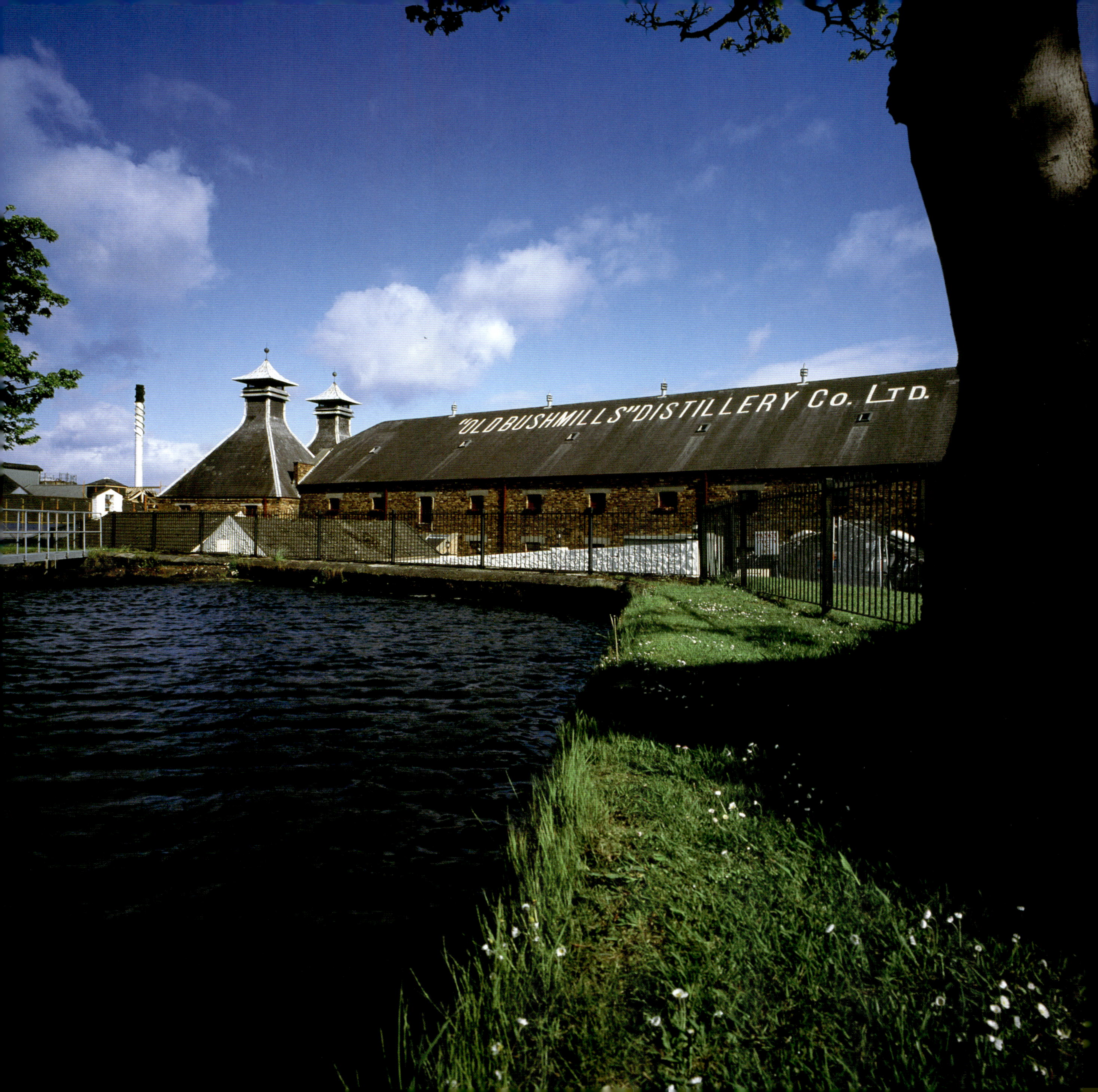
"OLD BUSHMILLS" DISTILLERY Co. LTD.

Chapter Twenty Six

Le Whiskey

In 1987 Bushmills launched their now world-famous ten-year-old single malt, but it was one of the few innovations that Irish Distillers had pioneered. The company was still hopelessly dependent on domestic sales; foreign markets were as elusive as ever and Seagram weren't getting the kind of returns they had expected.

It was no surprise when in May 1988 some of the largest players in the drinks business joined forces in an attempt to take over Irish Distillers. The GC&C consortium, so-called because the main players were Gilbey's (owners of Baileys), and soft drink company Cantrell & Cochrane (part owned by Guinness Ireland). Between them their parent companies owned eighteen of the world's Top 100 spirit brands. The consortium didn't pull its punches, saying that Irish Distillers' sales record was "a bloody embarrassment". Gilbey's went so far as to say that if Distillers had invented Baileys they wouldn't have known what to do with it. Their ambition was clear; 'Bushmills and Jameson should join the Top 100', and they clearly felt they were the people to make it happen.

The GC&C consortium wanted to break up Irish Distillers and share out the brands, "thereby ending the monopoly which has existed over the marketing of Irish whiskey since the early 1970s," as they put it. Gilbey's were to take Jameson, Paddy and Cork Dry Gin, while C&C were to own Tullamore Dew, Powers and Old Bushmills.

But Richard Burrows felt the GC&C bid of £3.15 a share undervalued Irish Distillers, so the board rejected the bid and the plan to parcel out the brands. As the takeover battle rumbled on, Burrows was in secret talks with the French company Pernod Ricard.

"I'd known Pernod Ricard for years through Austin Nichols, which is part of the group," said Richard Burrows. Austin Nichols are makers of Wild Turkey Kentucky whiskey

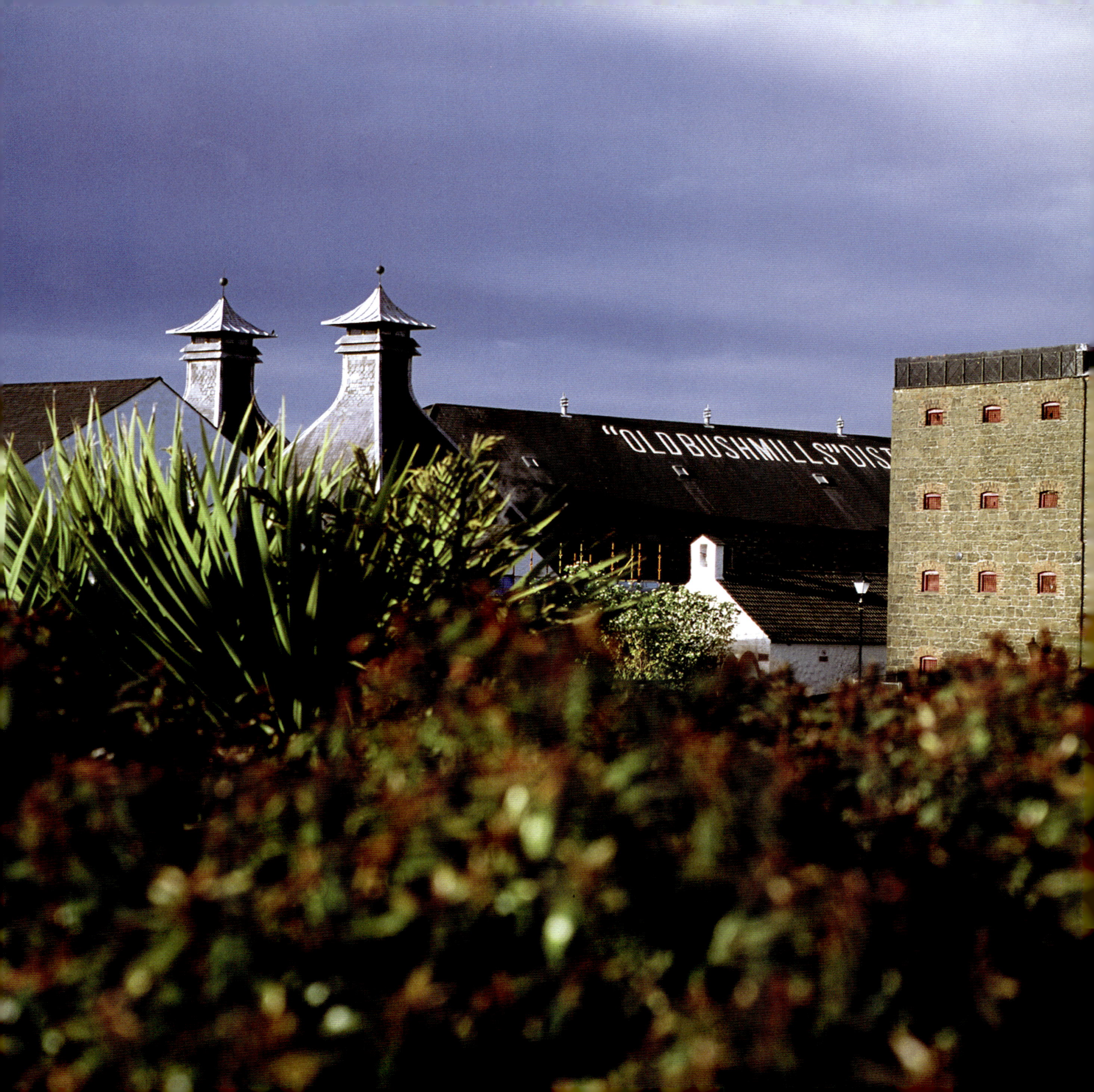
"OLD BUSHMILLS" DIST

and handled many Irish Distillers brands in the United States. "We were finding it difficult to get access to international markets and we were looking for a hook-up. It hadn't worked with Seagram's, and in the face of a hostile bid, Pernod Ricard were making the right noises."

Those 'noises' paid off, when the board of Irish Distillers and indeed the Irish government approved the take-over. The French had control of the Irish whiskey industry and set to work. Given the historic poor international sales, Pernod Ricard knew it would much easier to build a single brand, rather than several. Jameson was chosen over the likes of Powers, Paddy and even Old Bushmills, as Pernod poured their not inconsiderable talents into putting Irish whiskey back on the world stage. The gamble worked and sales of Jameson sales took off across the globe. By 1996 Jameson broke joined the world's top 100 spirits brands and cracked the magic one million cases a year barrier.

However, the success of Jameson came at a cost as Pernod Ricard dumped more and more niche brands, selling the likes of Tullamore Dew and simply dropping minor labels like Hewitts. During the 1990s life in Bushmills went on pretty much as before. More whiskies were laid down and older expressions were introduced, including a sixteen-year-old Malt in 1996 and a twenty-one-year-old in 2001, but the distillery always played second fiddle to Jameson.

OLD BUSHMILLS DISTILLERY
WHAT WE HAVE LOVED FOR CENTURIES, YOU WILL LOVE IN SECONDS.
Since 1608 it's been the same old story.
People love Old Bushmills the second they taste it.
Because Old Bushmills is smooth and mellow. A smoothness not easily come by.
The secret lies in an ancient process that goes back centuries to Ireland. To the village of Bushmills, and the oldest whiskey distillery in the world.
Here we pick the local barley ripe for harvest in nearby fields.
We draw clear water from the River Bush, water born for whiskey.
We commit these and other choice ingredients to our age-old triple distillation process.
Then our whiskey matures in handmade oaken casks.
When it finally comes of age years later, only then is it worthy of our label.
Old Bushmills.
But, like 18 generations before you, you'll know exactly what that means.
After your very first taste.
OLD BUSHMILLS
The taste you don't have to acquire.

Left and Above: US adverts from the 1980s

FOUR HUNDRED YEARS IN THE MAKING | 131

Why it's almost blasphemous to drink anything but Bushmills on St. Patrick's Day.

To a Bushmills drinker, the facts of the matter are undeniable.

First fact: St. Patrick himself lived "a mere stone's throw away" from our distillery (the oldest in the world).

Second fact: *Someone* spread the word about our uncommonly smooth whiskey (it's triple-distilled).

<u>Hint</u>: Bushmills became popular in the very towns visited by St. Patrick.

Now. Knowing all this, how could *anyone* conceivably drink anything but Bushmills on St. Patrick's Day?

BUSHMILLS

Left and Above: US adverts from the 1980s

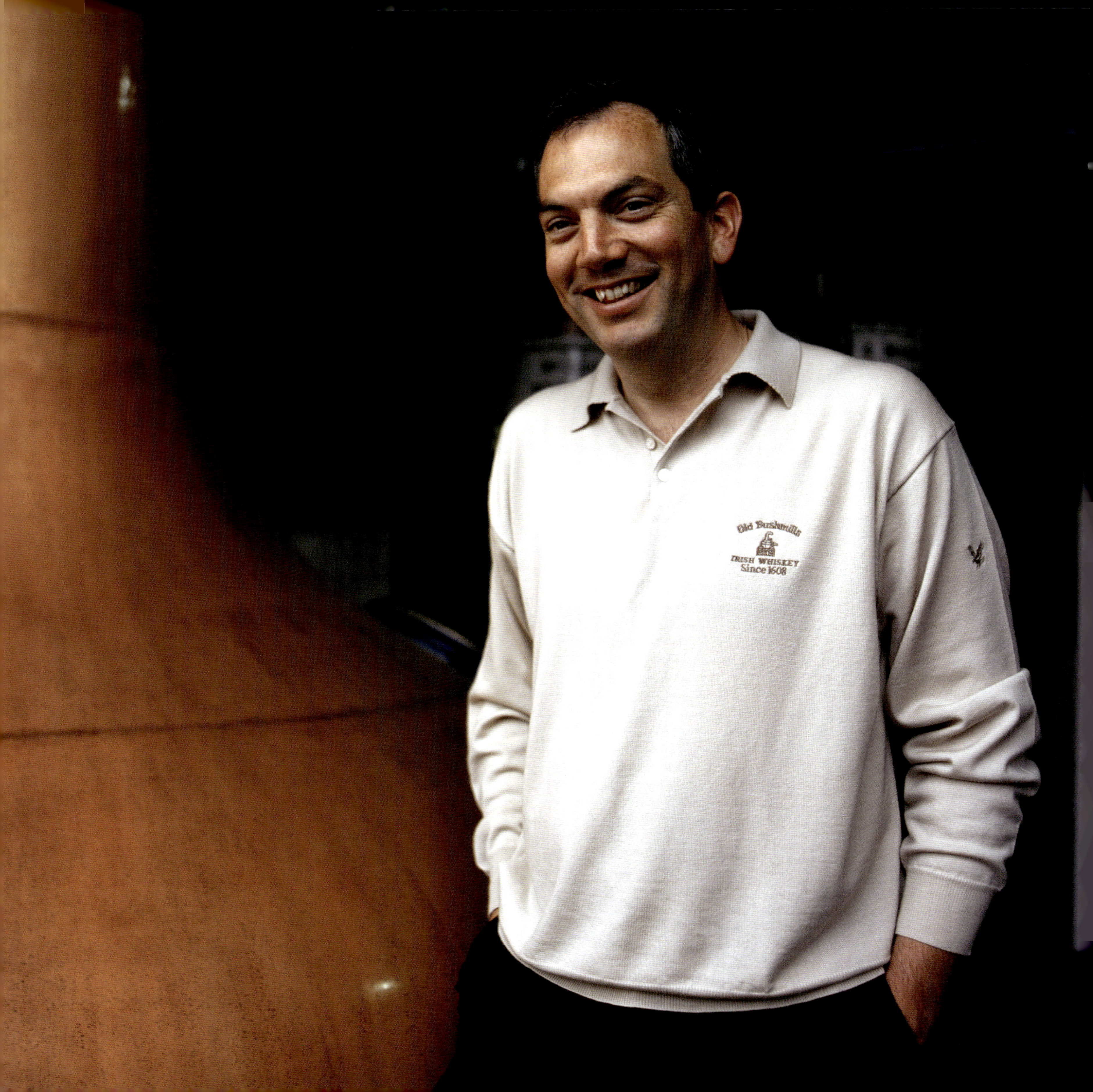
Old Bushmills
IRISH WHISKEY
Since 1608

Chapter Twenty Seven
New Frontier

There is only one certainty in the drinks industry – one company always seems to be taking over another. So it is not surprising that every now and then quirky things happen. In 2001 former Bushmills boss Richard Burrows led Pernod Ricard on a shopping trip that netted them Seagram. Ironically Irish Distillers ended up being part of the team who took over the company that helped it take over Old Bushmills in the early 1970s.

In 2005 the Fates moved again. This time Pernod Ricard – by now the world's third largest drinks company, were after Allied Domecq, the second largest. It was a breathtakingly ambitious take-over, as Pernod was valued at some €3 billion less than its target. The only way it was going to work was if Diageo, the biggest of all was offered a sacrifice to keep it out of the race for Allied Domecq. That offering was the Bushmills distillery, at the bargain price of £200 million.

"We engaged with them and did a deal," Burrows told the press at the time.

The deal paid off, the €10.95 billion merger went ahead and Diageo Chief Executive Paul Walsh was left with something he had always wanted – a major Irish whiskey brand to partner his other Irish-based success stories, Baileys and Guinness.

US Business magazine *Forbes* thought Diageo's deal was "truly platinum" while Ian Paisley Junior, the local Member of the Northern Ireland Assembly told the BBC, "if the brand develops and grows, then one would expect to see development at Bushmills and more job opportunities there."

Paisley was right: what this meant for Old Bushmills was radical. Bushmills' brands, so long kept in the shadow of Jameson, could now be pushed into the limelight. No sooner was the ink dry on the deal, than Diageo started to pump money into the distillery and began ramping up

Left: Full steam ahead. Bushmills' new ambitions mean Colum and his team have never been busier.

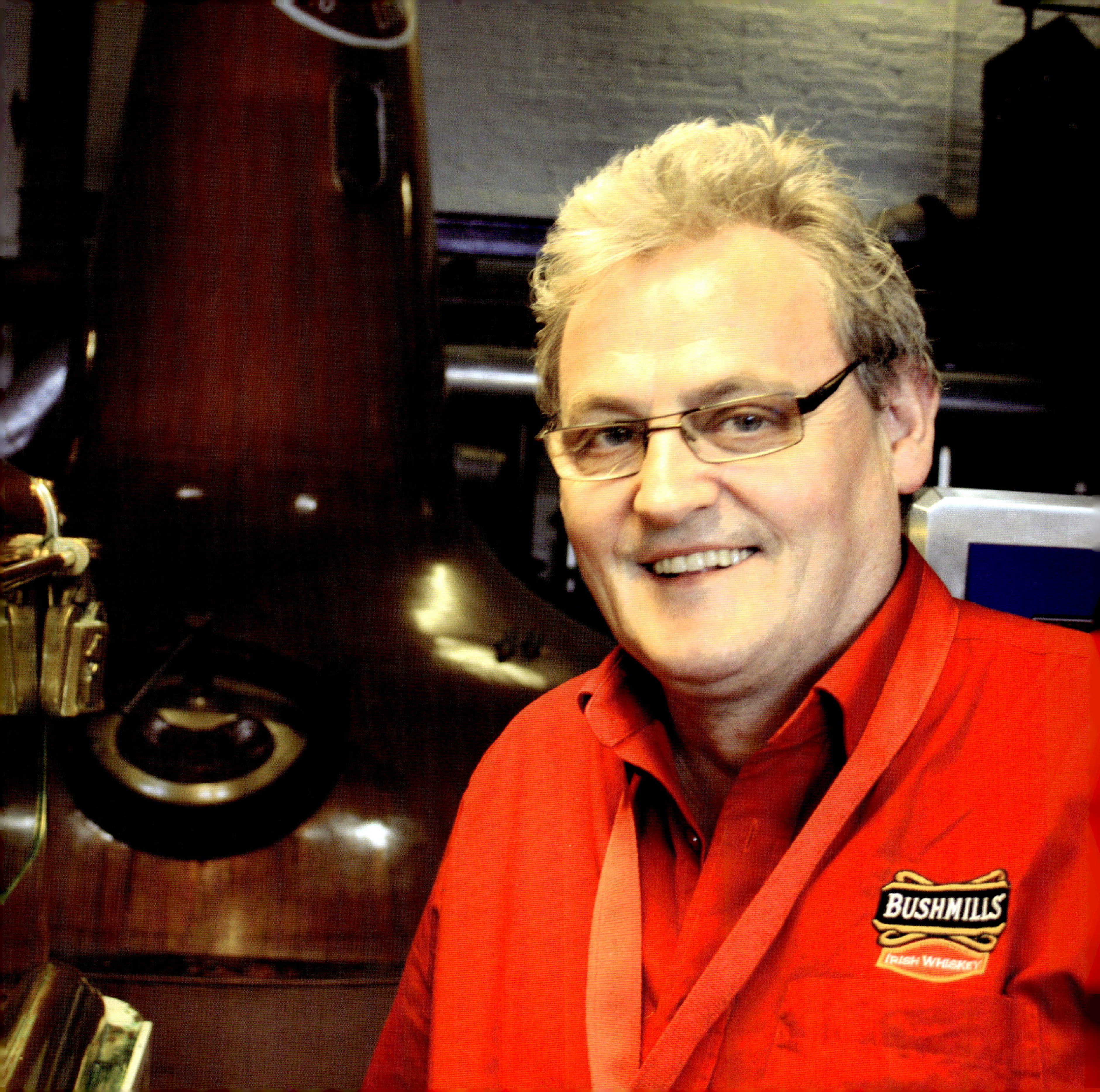
BUSHMILLS
IRISH WHISKEY

production. In 2005 Bushmills was selling some 400,000 cases of whiskey; within two years that had grown to 500,000. Walsh aims to grow sales further to 1 million cases by 2011, taking a chunk out of Jameson's dominance of the Irish whiskey sector.

Over three years some £6 million was invested in production and marketing Old Bushmills. New anniversary packaging was introduced, the company started sponsoring the Irish Rugby team and the brand launched its first ever global advertising push. This refreshingly honest campaign brought to life the people, the place and the craft of the distillery, with a series of photographs featuring the workers who actually make the whiskey.

But producing "Irish at its Best" takes a lot of time and planning and with the sales curve in mind, it fell to Gordon Donoghue, the distillery Supply Director to implement the kind of change needed to supply future demand, so Donoghue pretty much doubled output immediately after the acquisition. Three day weeks became five day weeks, as he and Master Distiller Colum Egan slowly but surely steered the distillery towards 24/7 production.

Whiskey making is a delicated time consuming operation and keeping standards high while almost trebling production is no small task. Quality is of course the first concern, and with the distillery already running at full capacity the team at Bushmills had to handle the inevitable expansion carefully.

Above: Master Distiller Colum Egan
Left: Stillman Kenny Garvin joined Bushmills in September 1979. His grandfather Thomas was foreman in the malt barn (1920-61). His father Ronald was a joiner (1968-88) and his mother was one of the first ladies to work in the bottling hall (1969-85).

FOUR HUNDRED YEARS IN THE MAKING | 137

138 | BUSHMILLS

The whole whiskey making process had to be reassessed and expanded without ruining the character of the building or the whiskey.

First up was a new mash tun, but that caused a bottleneck in the already crowded still house and this would be harded to remedy. A new still was needed, but where to put it? The Victorian still house is home to four wash-stills and five spirit-stills and over the past century or so expansion had been steady, but manageable. Increasing production threefold in three years was uncharterd territory and with the public having access to each and every stage of production, any further changes would have to be carefully considered.

A new still scheduled for installation in the anniversary summer of 2008 is the tenth in an already crowded space; it will have to be lowered through the roof.

Work is also in progress on a new warehouse, number 17, which will be used to mature all the new whiskey and 400 years after the original licence to distil, Bank of Ireland released a new series of bank notes featuring the distillery – Old Bushmills has never been busier.

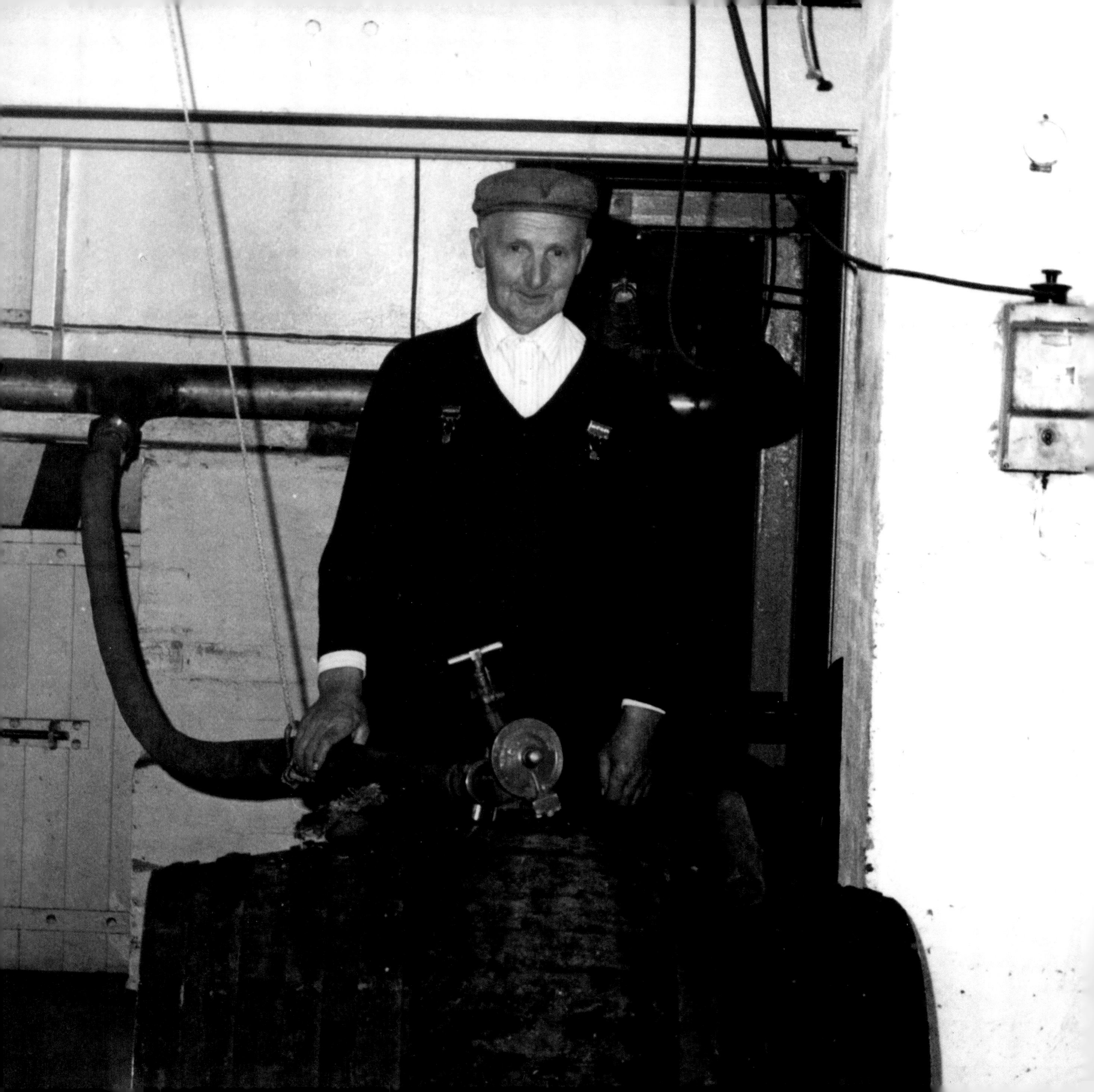

Chapter Twenty Eight

Memories

For six people, the 400th anniversary of the licence to distil marked another significant anniversary. For the '1608 Club', it was the year they retired.

These six are typical of generations of workers who have seen so much change. They started their careers working for a family firm and ended as part of the largest drinks company in the world. During their lives at Old Bushmills, the whiskey industry changed beyond recognition, but these were the people who made that change possible. These are the people who help make Old Bushmills great.

In the 1960s whiskey making would only begin late in the year after the barley had been harvested, and would continue until the early summer. However most of the workers were kept on full time. Billy Chambers recalls that during the summer they would do repair jobs around the place.

"I remember we'd paint the place, and one year I was on the roof painting the lettering!"

Needless to say these were the days before Health and Safety forms and hazard assessments.

"Sure it was dangerous," added Billy, "but that's just the way things were in those days."

One of the biggest changes has been in the way people end up working at the distillery. Up until the 1970s people got jobs in the Bushmills distillery under recommendation.

"If you knew a lad wanted a job, you'd ask around. See if they were all right," remembers Billy, whose father worked at the distillery, and whose daughter is now the Brand Home Manager.

"But that's nothing unusual: you can get three or four generations of uncles, fathers, sons and daughters working here. I went to work at the distillery for three months," he added, "and ended up staying for 43 years!"

Over the years the distillery has been a great source of employment in an area with little industrial development. As

Left: It runs in the family: Billy Chambers' father David worked at Bushmills before him (here filling casks, 1973)

late as the mid-1960s there were 16 coopers at Bushmills and another 3 in Coleraine. A couple of coopers would be started every few years as it took a long time to learn all the skills, such as how to move a 600 kg butt without doing in your back. Nowadays Watson McCook is the distillery's last remaining cooper. Watson has worked at Bushmills all his life, and like so many of his generation, he is due to retire very soon.

With over 200 years' experience between them, there is not much that the 1608 Club have not seen. Ronnie Brennan started working at Coleraine distillery in 1964 and he remained there, on and off until the place finally closed in 1979. In fact Ronnie did the last mash in Coleraine.

"I was sorry to see it close," he said. "But you do your job and get on with it. It was sad, but the move to Old Bushmills suited me. You see I live in Bushmills, and having to drive to Coleraine every day was a real pain!"

Ronnie was also the last person to work the old mash tun in Bushmills. This has since been sliced open and can be seen during the distillery tour.

"I didn't just wear out one mash tun," he laughed. "I wore out two!"

When it comes to not doing things by halves, Ronnie is not alone. Billy Chambers has emptied two distilleries. He picked up the last load of grain whiskey from the closed Coleraine distillery in the 1980s and brought it to the Bushmills warehouses and before that he helped clear out Killowen.

Right: Uel Thompson, stillman, joined Bushmills in 1973

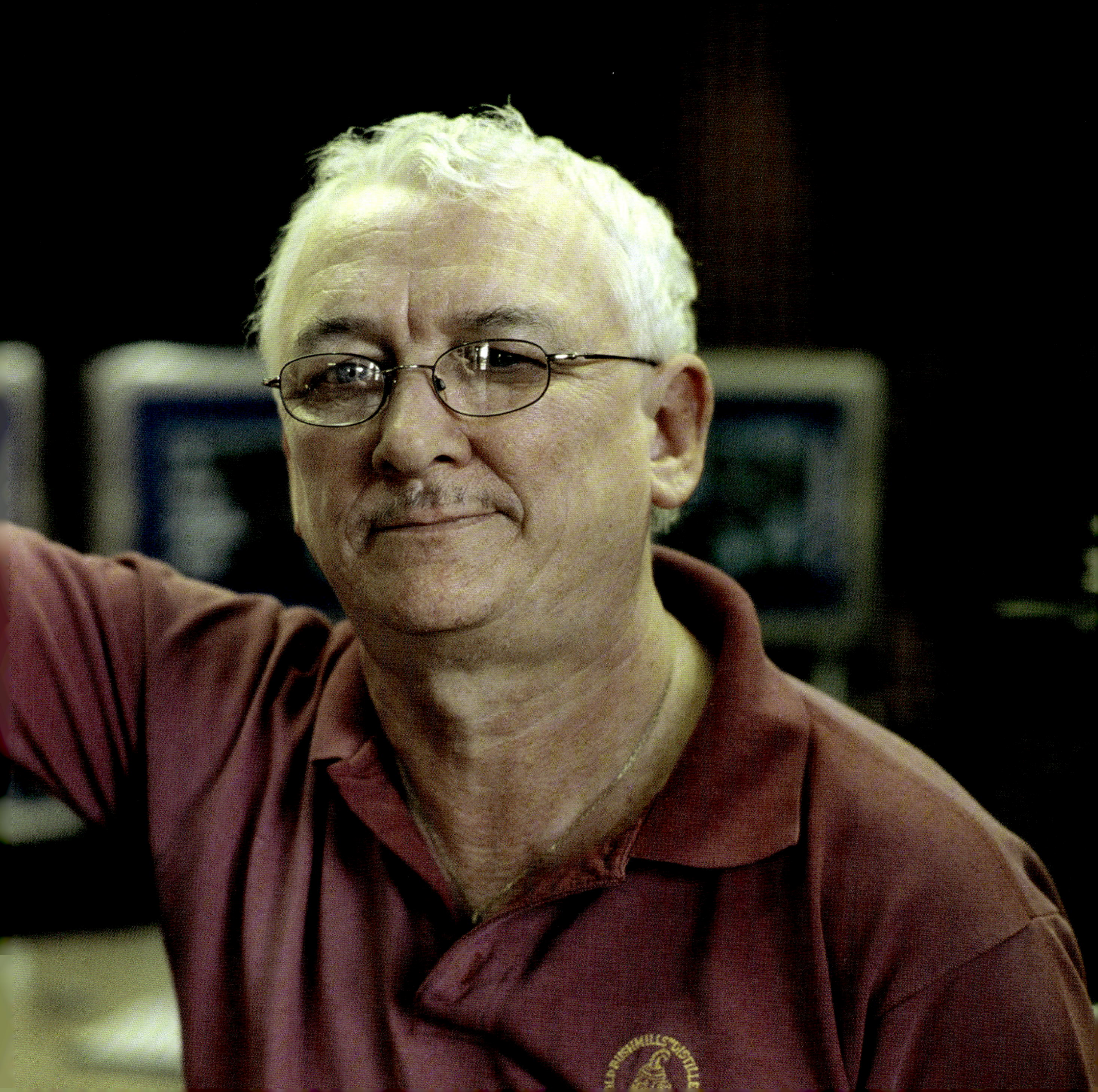

Right: Harry Elliott, maturation foreman, joined Bushmills in 1976
Above: Taking a water sample from the distillery dam for analysis in the lab. A bit of science before the magic begins.

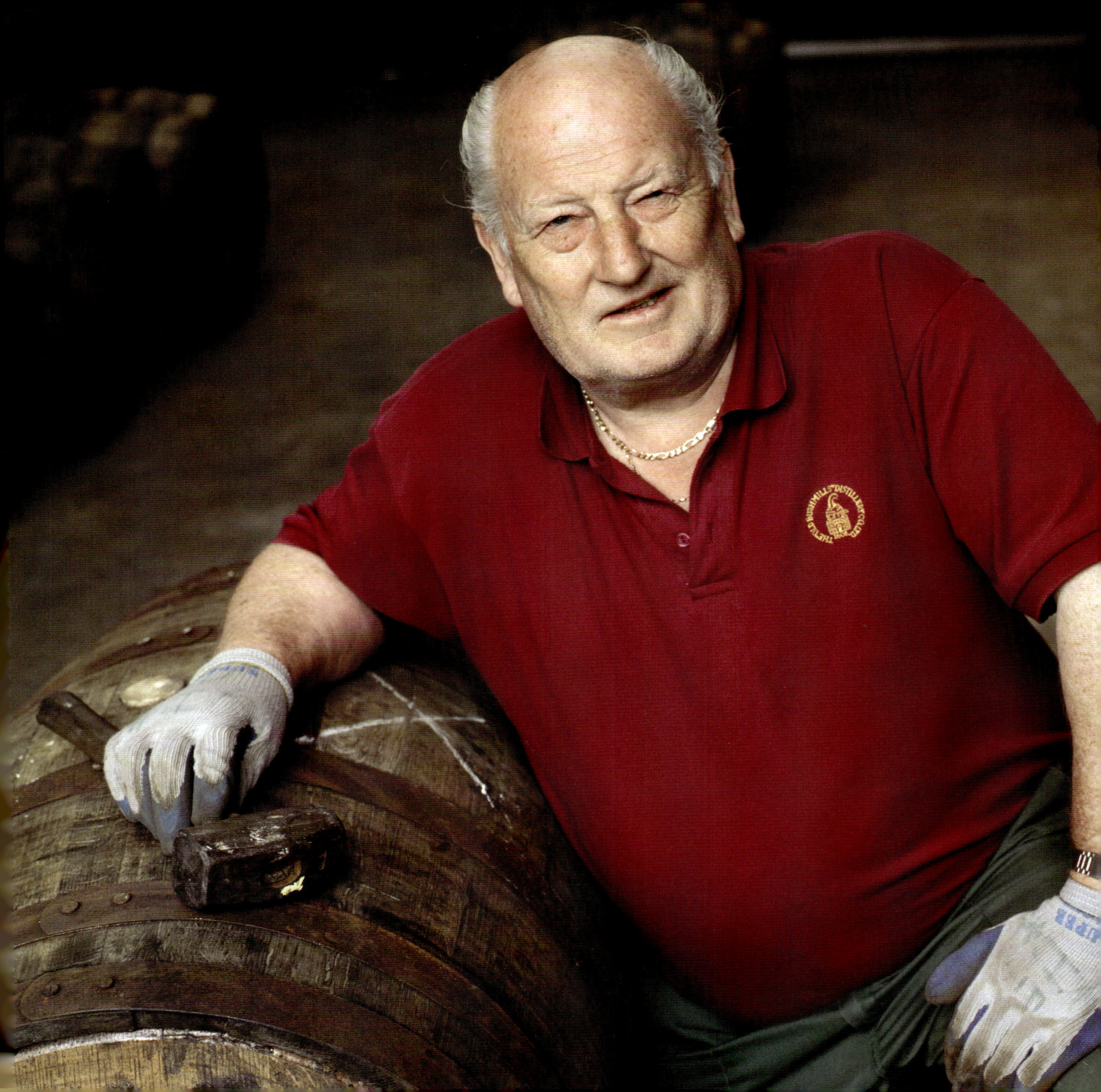

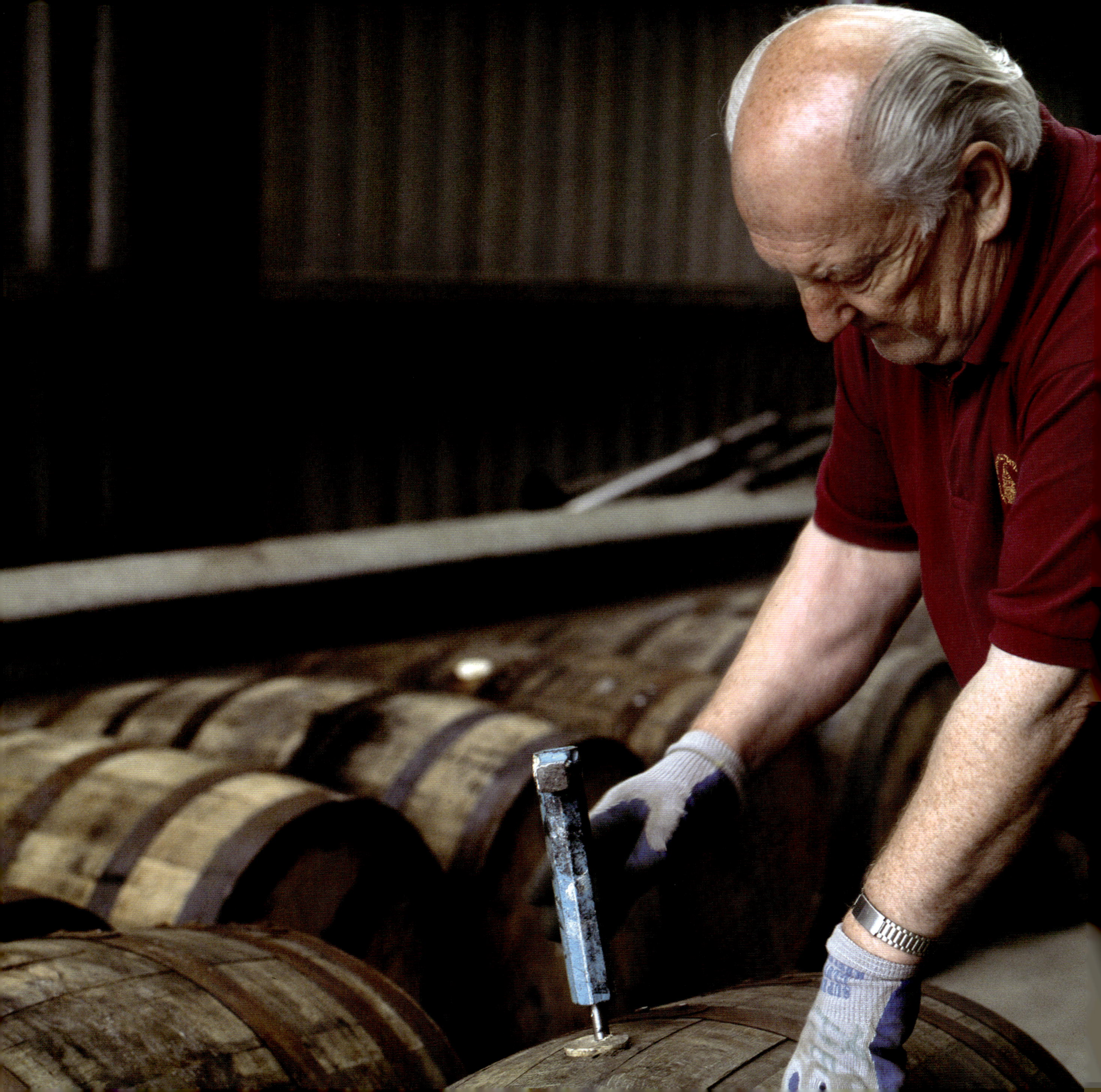

"After they sold off Killowen, it would have been the early '70s, I remember filling my truck with the last casks. I had to drive down a one-way street, but I did permission from the police!"

Harry Elliott spent 43 years working in maturation, and who would therefore know a thing or two about ageing spirit. He remembers tasting some of that whiskey. It had matured on the damp floor of the old warehouse. There was no concrete under the casks, just pressed earth.

"Oh, it made for fine whiskey," he remembered. "It would have been malt, it was an old one from Coleraine and perfectly matured. These old warehouses were something special."

As well as the old damp warehouses of Killowen, warehouse number 7 at Bushmills had a fine reputation for producing exceptional whiskey. It is said, that in warehouse number 2 at Old Bushmills, you can still see the traditional old flooring, and it is a great place to do a whiskey tasting when the spirit is drawn straight from the barrel!

Molly Anderson and Bellina McMullen each worked on the bottling line at Bushmills for 34 years. They remembered when the bottling was moved from Coleraine.

"In those days we had to hand label everything," recalled Molly. "We'd put the label on, then hold it up to the light to make sure it was straight."

When the bottling started at Bushmills, Bellina remembers getting to grips with her new job.

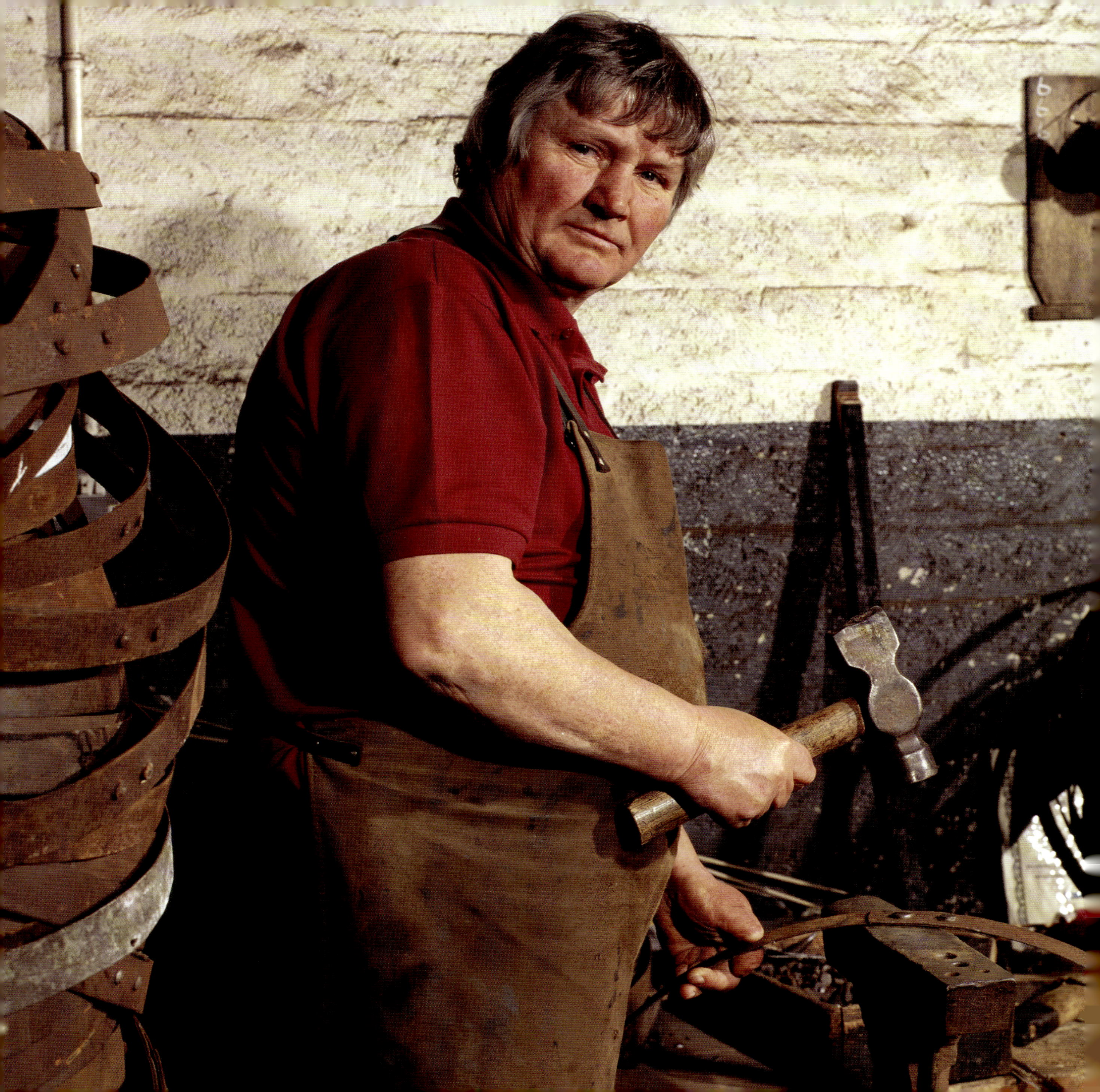

"I remember breaking a bottle by mistake and everyone saying it would be taken out of my wages. Then I accidentally broke the glass measure used by the Customs Office and I thought, 'Oh what's *that* going to cost me!?'"

Things certainly have changed: these days the bottling line is fully automated and every drop of whiskey is electronically accounted for. That was not always the way. There was a time when every employee would queue up at the end of the day for a "wee nip" – a shot of whiskey.

"You'd have to line up for it," said Billy, "but some of the cheeky lads would get their shot, then join the end of the queue and try again. If they were told they had already got their whiskey, they'd reply saying 'No, that was yesterday'!"

Eventually the daily dram was done away with and replaced by a glass of lemonade. That did not go down too well.

"Lemonade is fine," Ronnie recounted dourly, "but only as a mixer!"

After a while the lemonade too was done away with and instead, every now and then, workers would get a wee bottle to take away.

"I recall someone, who will remain nameless…" smiled Billy, "and he shoved the bottle into his back pocket, but then slipped and fell on his backside. When he stood up he felt something wet running down his leg and said, 'I hope that's blood!'"

There have been a lot of changes at Old Bushmills over the past four hundred years, yet the more things change, the more they stay the same. In the reception area (where Harry and his pals used to practice bowling) you will find a bottle of Old Bushmills Single Malt. But this is no ordinary Old Bushmills – it dates from 1888 and is the company's oldest surviving bottle.

Not long after his arrival, Master Distiller Colum Egan got a long needle and took a small sample from the bottle and sent it for analysis. This whiskey would have been made during the reign of Queen Victoria, the same whiskey that won Gold at the Paris Exhibition the year the Eiffel Tower was unveiled. Surprisingly, it is pretty much the same ten-year-old malt you can buy today. Perhaps that says all that needs to be said about the consistency of Old Bushmills:

You don't get to be the best because you're the oldest; you get to be the oldest because you are the best.

Left: Watson McCook joined Bushmills as an apprentice cooper in 1966. Bushmills is one of only a few whiskey distilleries to keep an on-site cooperage to this day.

Right: Over 200 years of experience at Bushmills between them (from left to right, top to bottom) the '1608 Club': John Black, Harry Elliott, Ronnie Brennan, Molly Anderson, Billy Chambers, Bellina McMullen

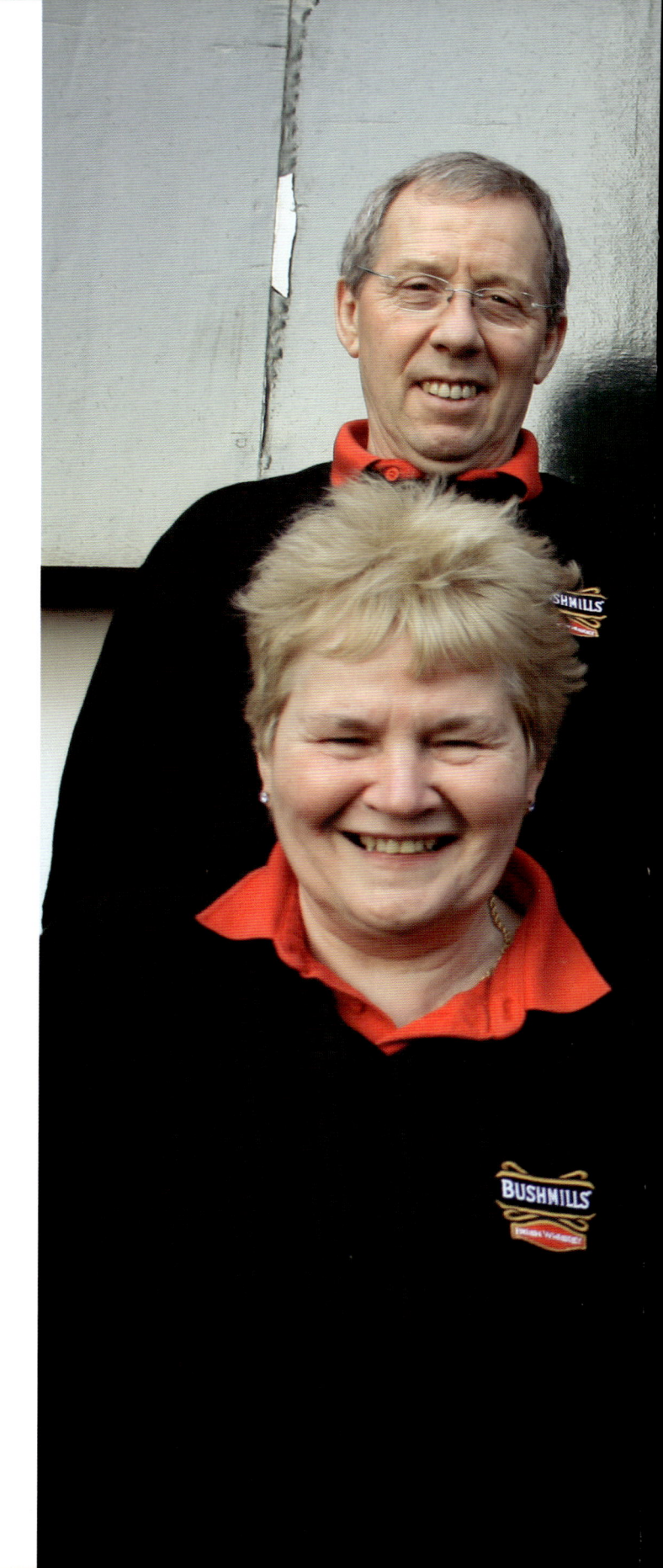

BUSHMILLS
IRISH WHISKEY
BUSHMILLS
IRISH WHISKEY
BUSHMILLS
IRISH WHISKEY

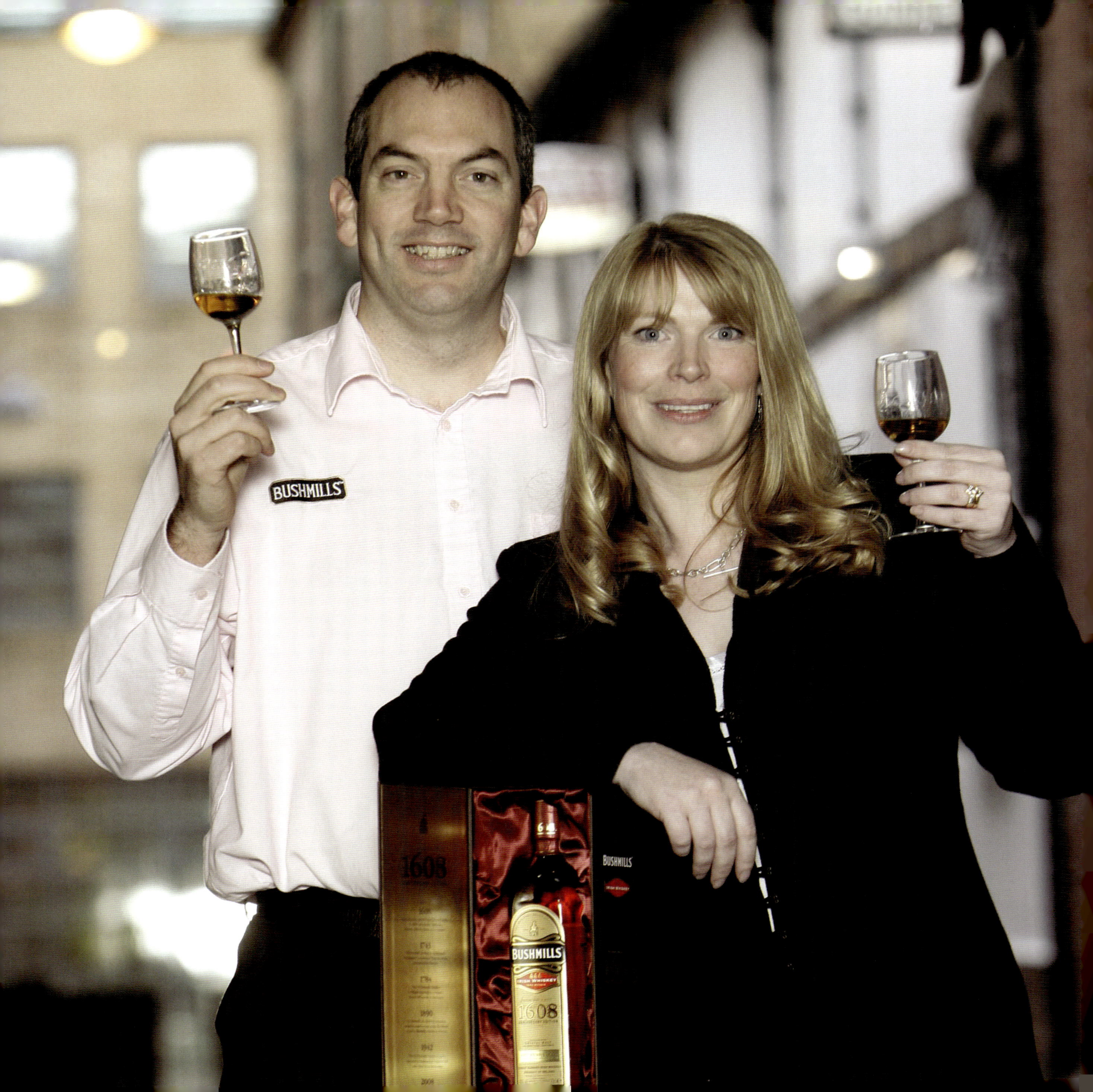
BUSHMILLS
1608
BUSHMILLS
BUSHMILLS
1608

Left: Let's raise a glass.... Colum Egan and Helen Mulholland toast 400 years of Whiskey-making heritage with their new creation, Bushmills 1608.

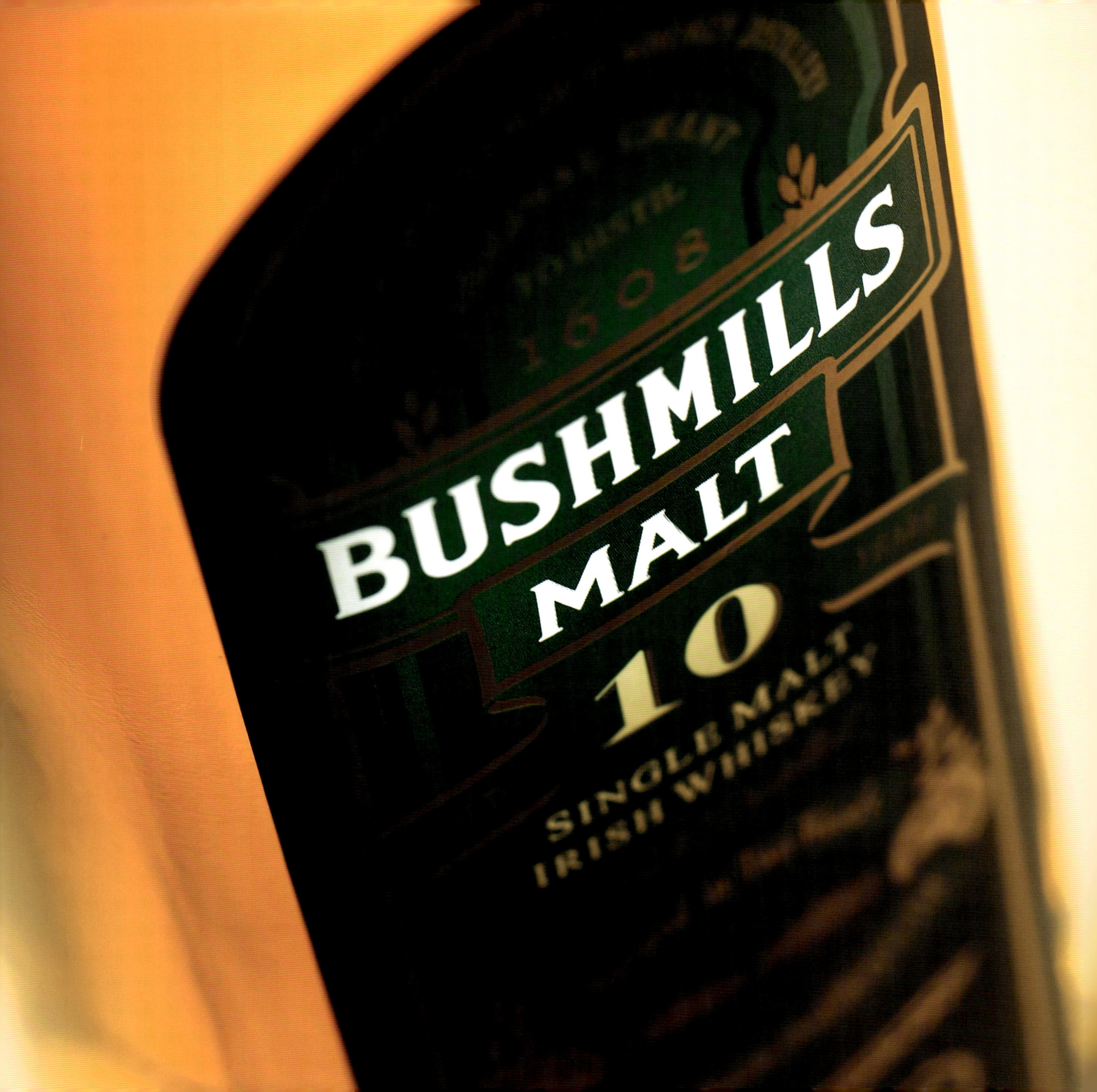
1608
BUSHMILLS
MALT
10
SINGLE MALT
IRISH WHISKEY

Chapter Twenty Nine
The Drink

If you were to build a distillery from scratch it would not look anything like Old Bushmills. This higgledy-piggledy collection of red brick and slate is full of character, but these listed buildings are all that remain of an earlier age of red brick, water wheels and steam.

New uses have to be found for old buildings and any expansion has to be done sensitively. You cannot afford to sacrifice the charm that made Old Bushmills special in the first place.

There needs to be living space for Peter the Pheasant, who escaped from a nearby shooting estate and found sanctuary in the distillery grounds, and creative space for Liz to create classics like the to-die-for Bushmills Cheesecake she makes for the visitors café.

It is an eccentric place. The trick then is to make the best of what is there, while keeping in mind what is really important – the character of the whiskey itself. So in the past hundred years, while a lot of things have changed, it is the attention to detail that continues to make Old Bushmills whiskey so special.

For a start, then as now Old Bushmills whiskey has always been made from the same three things:

Water, yeast and malted barley. That's the chemistry.

I like to add a fourth item to the list: Time. That's the *magic*.

Left: 10 Year Old Single Malt

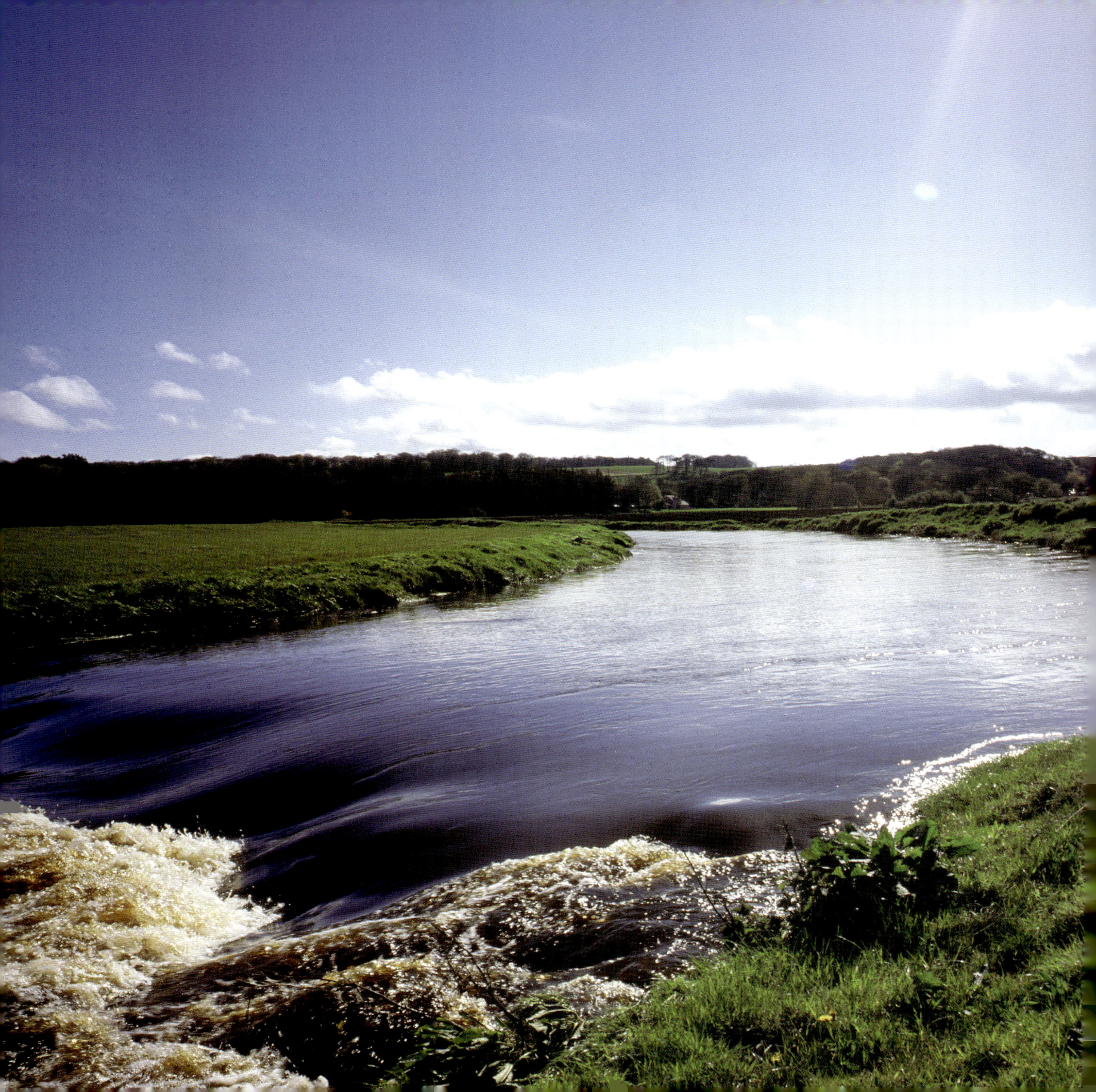

Water

Water is easy. It is everywhere. If you are visiting Co. Antrim, bring an umbrella because it won't be long before you will need to use it. There is a joke that around here even the sheep have webbed feet. But we have to be thankful for all this rain, because without it there would be no whiskey. That is because the water used in the making of Old Bushmills has always come from the same source, St Columb's Rill, a small stream and a tributary to the River Bush, which flows through the distillery grounds. The water from this stream is gathered in a pool outside the distillery, before being pumped inside, where the *magic* can begin.

Yeast

For something quite amazing, yeast is pretty dull. It is kind of a crumbly butter coloured cake, but it is a living organism, and it just loves sugar. Yeast is the magic ingredient that gives us two very useful by-products: alcohol, without which there would be no beer or whiskey; and CO_2, without which we would have only flat bread.

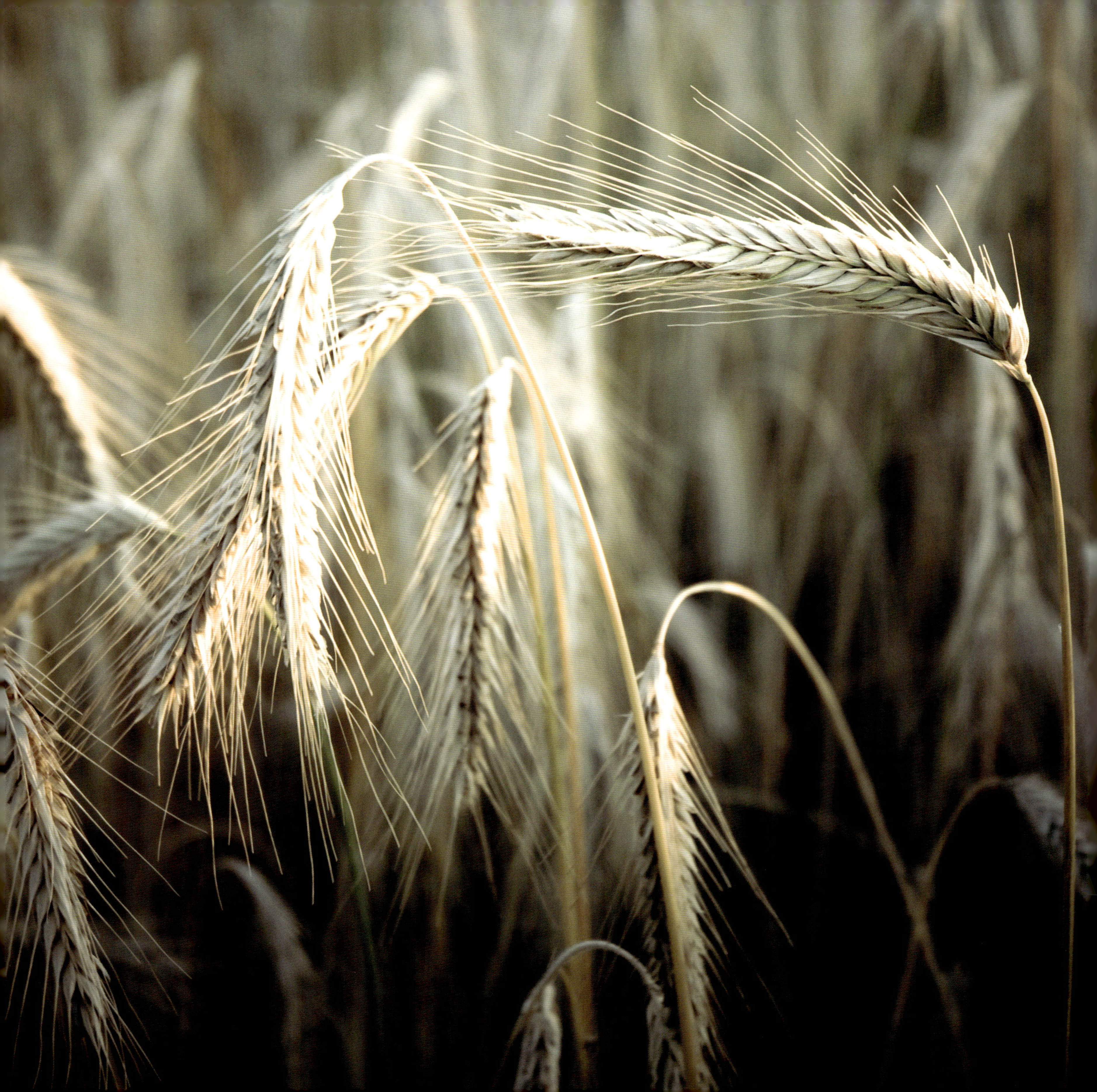

Malted Barley

Barley is a grain. It looks a bit like wheat and it thrives in the cooler, damp climates of Ireland and Scotland.

Malt then is the third and final ingredient needed to make whiskey. Malted barley is simply barley that has been allowed to sprout. To make malt you need to confuse the barley into thinking that spring has arrived. The barley is soaked in water then kept nice and warm. It's like a perfect May week in Ireland: the conditions are ideal for growing, and after 4 to 5 days the barley starts to germinate.

What happens is that the cell walls break down, and the long strings of starch shorten to become simple sugars. This is the food which the plant will need to grow, but this is also the sugar we need to make whiskey. So the germination has to be stopped before the tiny seed starts 'eating itself'.

For all our science, the malting process is still very intuitive. It takes the considerable skills of the maltster to know when to stop the germination. Usually this is when the rootlet is around the same length as the grain.

A blast of heat is the best way to stop germination in its tracks, and what you use to generate that heat will affect the final flavour of the whiskey. Nowadays Irish barley is malted in large rotating drums using hot dry air, but that was not always the case.

Until 1972 Bushmills had its own maltings (now the distillery café – did I mention the cheesecake?). Here the fire that would dry the barley was started with peat that was dug locally and carried to the distillery. Once the fire was going, coal would be used; this meant that the barley was only exposed to peat smoke for a brief time. Ronnie Brennan, who worked at the distillery during this period, said it gave the whiskey a "very soft taste".

During the mid-1970s Irish Distillers, who owned the plant then, experimented with a very heavily peated malt, but according to Ronnie it just didn't work. The whiskey made at Old Bushmills does not need to get its flavour from 'peat reek'.

Two different kinds of whiskey come into play at Bushmills.

First up are Single Malts: the ten-year-old, the sixteen-year-old and the twenty-one-year-old. These are made, matured and bottled on site. Bushmills is the only place in Ireland that does this.

Then there are the blends: Bushmills Original, Black Bush and 1608. These are made by blending malt and grain whiskeys. Grain whiskey has never been produced at Bushmills; it used to be made at Coleraine. Today Bushmills sources grain whiskey from Midleton. Staff at Bushmills insist that they only source grain 'spirit' from Midleton, distilled to their own specification, to be casked at Bushmills, technically becoming Irish whiskey only after 3 years at the Co. Antrim distillery.

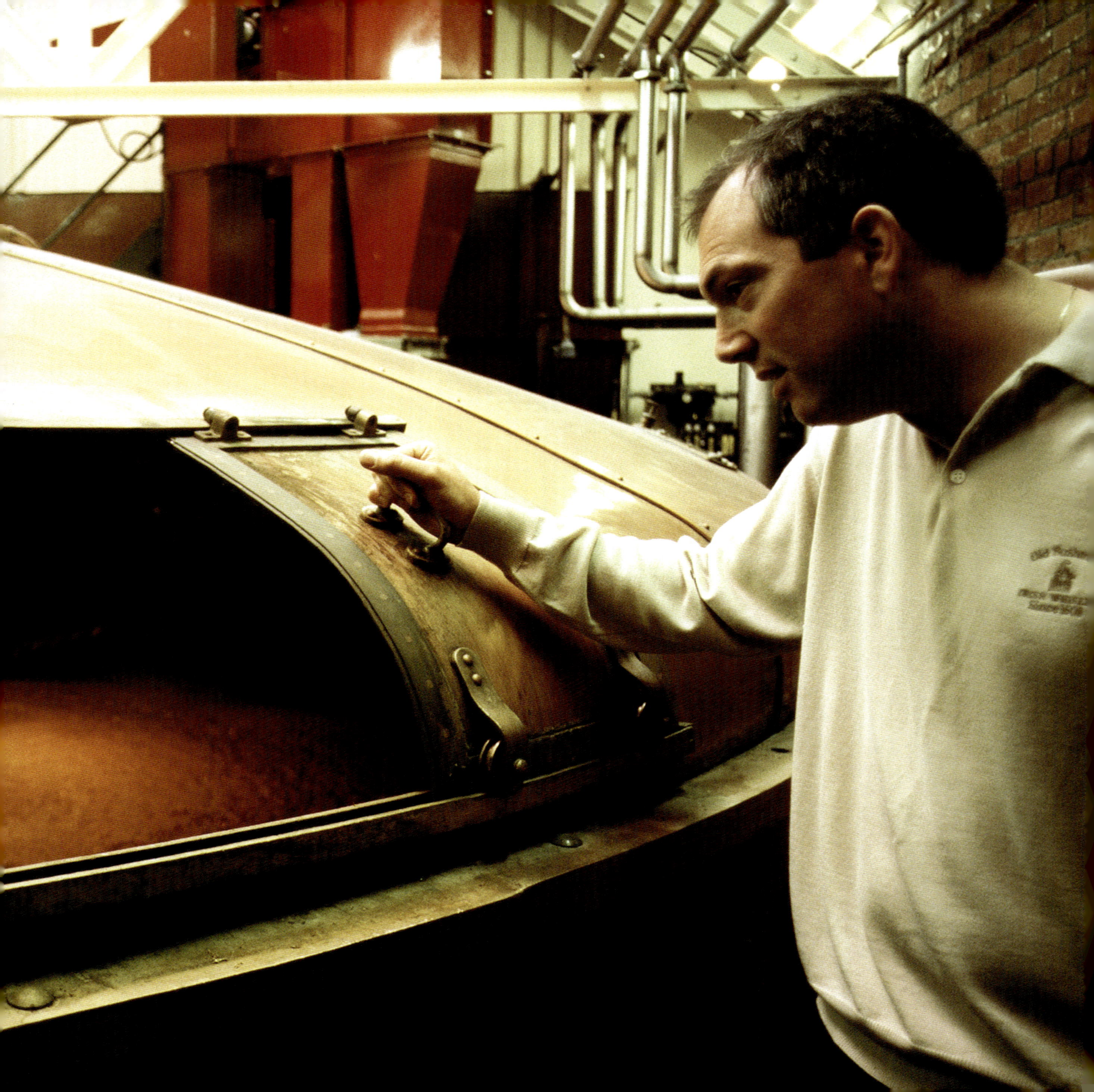

Chapter Thirty

How to Make Whiskey

Colum Egan is the Old Bushmills Master Distiller and a man who knows a lot about whiskey and a lot about how to manage his team.

"It takes six guys to make our whiskey; that's two per shift. One guy mashes, and one guy runs the still house – that's three shifts over twenty-four hours, so it's a six-man team. The least experienced of these guys has been doing it for 25 years, the most experienced has been at it for 43 years. So these guys know what they're doing. People ask me 'What happens when you leave the distillery?' I tell them, well, if they don't know how to make it after 25 years, we're in trouble."

1. Mashing

The name says everything: *mashing*. When you look inside the mash tun that Ronnie Brennan finally 'wore out' after 40 years of service, you get a real idea of what is involved in this part of the whiskey making process. It is basically a large saucepan with built in stirrers.

Before the malt is cooked, it is put into a mill and ground into a *grist* (thus the expression 'grist to the mill'). Ten tonnes of this grist and a load of hot water are emptied into the mash tun, and from then it is a bit like making watery porridge. In this process you do not want the cooked grain: you want the cloudy water, which since everything needs a name, is now called *wort*.

This wort is drained off, then the process is repeated twice. Each time the water gets hotter and hotter, as more and more *maltose* is extracted. You may well get a hint of peaches in the air if you are in the mash house at this time. If not they'll have some fine Antrim air for you to breathe, so don't worry.

The three loads of wort are then pumped away – they will go on and become whiskey. The cooked grist or *draff* is taken away and dried – this will go on to be cattle food. Nothing

Left: "What's cooking?" Colum Egan takes a look inside the mash tun where the ground barley malt is mixed with hot water to extract the cereal's natural sugars. This old mash tun was replaced in 2007.

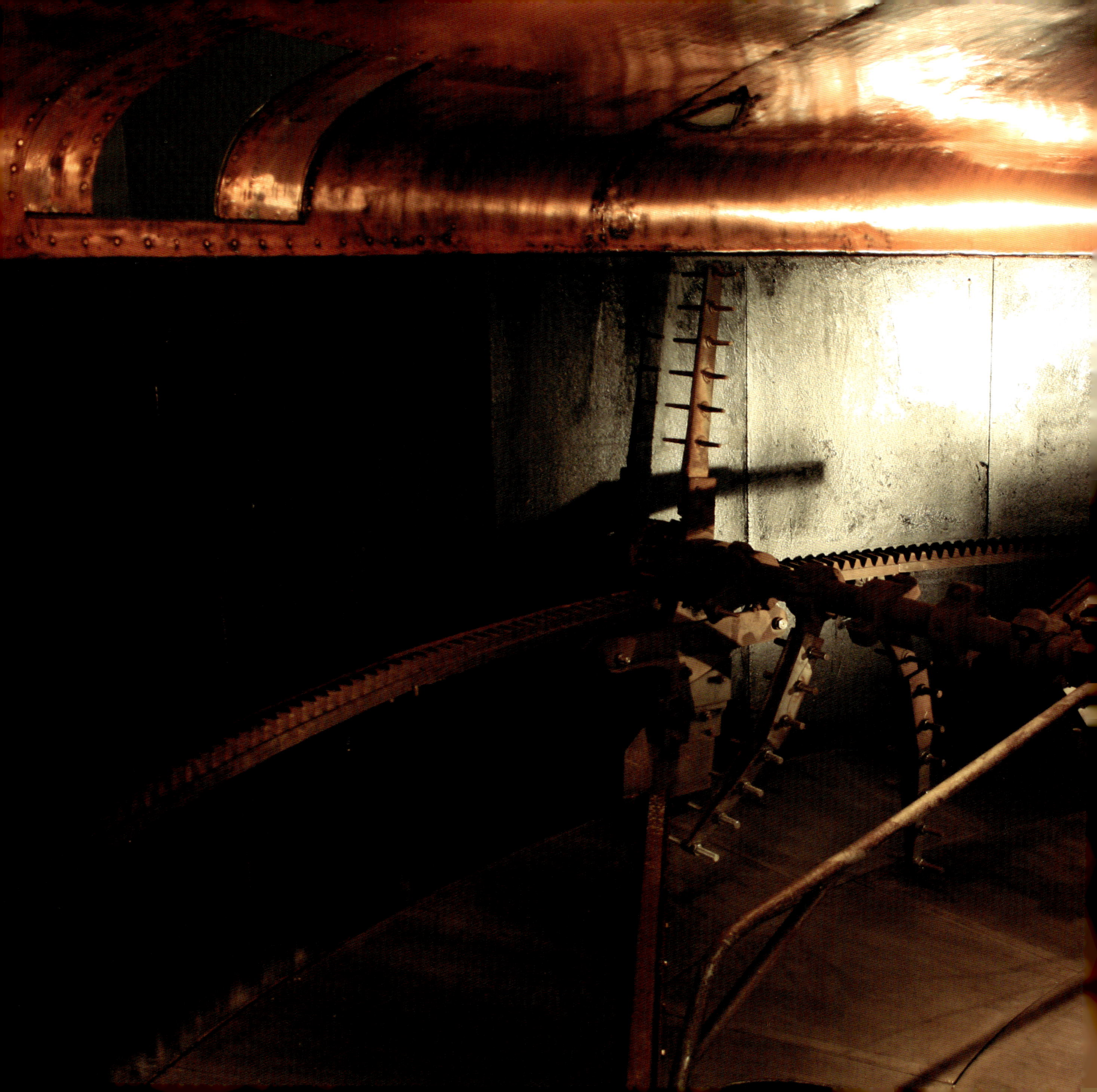

Left: Inside the old mash tun. Made of cast iron with a copper lid, it was replaced in 2007 by a larger and more efficient stainless steel version to increase Bushmills' distilling capacity.

No 2 WASH STILL
CONTENTS
15,920 LITRES
WASH STILL
CONTENTS
LITRES

here is wasted, and if the distillery is lucky they can sometimes sell this draff for more than they paid for the malt, but don't say I told you so.

2. Fermentation

The wort is now a sweet-tasting, milky looking water. It appears to be pretty uninspiring stuff. This is pumped into another large stainless vat called a *wash back*, where yeast is added. This is where the first magical transformations happen.

Over a period of 59 hours, the yeast consumes the simple sugars in the wort, and you are left with something resembling a sweet-smelling warm beer. This *wash* is pretty strong stuff too, at around 7.5% abv (alcohol by volume). It won't get any stronger though, as the alcohol in the wash will eventually kill the very yeast that brought it into existence. So to get a more alcoholic spirit, we need to distil.

3. Distillation

The still room is where chemistry and art collide.

The science bit is easy. Alcohol has a lower boiling point than water, so if you heat the wash, the alcohol will evaporate first. Collect that and the job is done.

I told you it was simple! It took two lines to explain the chemistry; the art though will take a lot longer. It is all about variables: from the size of the still; to its shape; from how it is fired to the cat that sleeps underneath it.

"His name is 'Ginger', or 'Whiskey' or whatever comes to mind!" Kenny Garvin operates the stills and feeds the distillery cat that spends a lot of its life curled up by a nice warm still. "He's like myself – he's 'third generation'," he joked. "His grandfather worked here with my grandfather. Take him away and the whiskey just wouldn't taste the same!"

Apart from telling tall tales, the art of the still man is to separate the good stuff from the not-so-good stuff. The exact moment to collect the run and the exact moment to stop cannot be learnt from a book. It takes a keen eye and a steady hand to produce the kind of new-make spirit that will one day carry the Old Bushmills name.

At Bushmills, whiskey is distilled three times. The first pass happens in a wash still.

Kenny MacAuley has been an engineer at Bushmills for over 40 years, and he knows every last washer in the still house.

"The stills used to be heated by coal fires lit underneath, but that stopped in 1965."

Up until this, the stills had flat tops to accommodate the *rummagers* inside. Rummagers were basically automated stirrers operated by a cog, and they kept the wash moving so it did not burn over the direct heat. When the distillery changed to heating the wash with internal steam jets, the rummagers were skipped, but stills were kept until the mid-1990s, when they were replaced by more elegant ones with swan necks rather than flat tops.

The science remains the same. The liquid that comes from the first distillation is around 25% abv, the second pass raises this to 70%, but it is the third and final distillation that makes Bushmills so special.

No one knows when or why the Irish started distilling their whiskey for a third time. It is pretty unusual, as in most parts of the world whisky is distilled just twice. But one thing is certain: the third pass through the still is crucial to the flavour profile of Old Bushmills. The third distillation produces a lighter, purer spirit at around 83% abv. Scotch takes a lot of its flavour from peat, while Bourbon and Tennessee Whiskey rely a lot on new oak barrels for their flavour profile. But when you take a sip of anything from Old Bushmills, you will

Left: Inside the still house. Catching a glimpse of five of Bushmills' nine stills. A tenth still will come in the summer of 2008 to help cope with increasing demand for Bushmills whiskeys.

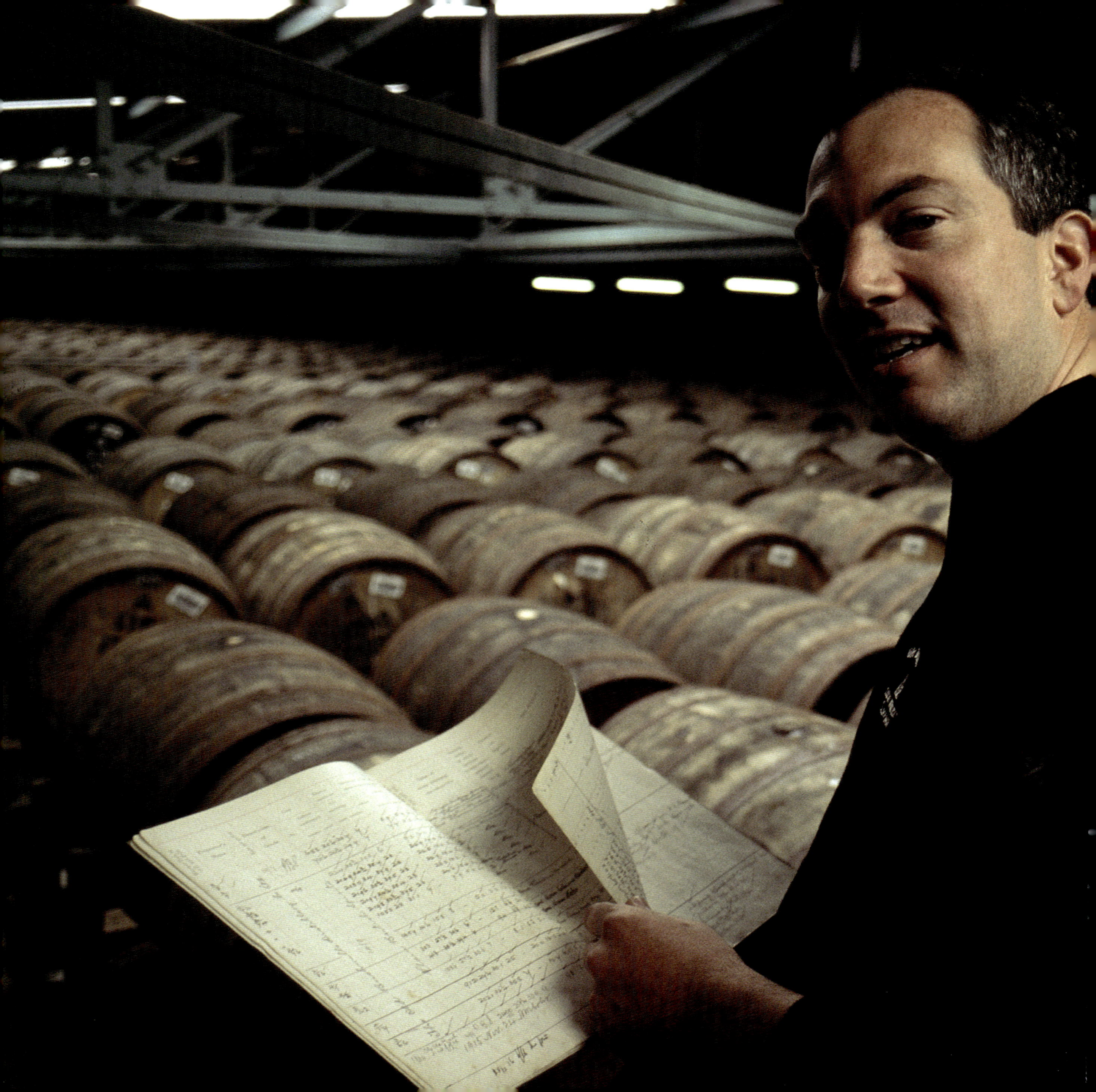

taste the whiskey, and most of that flavour will come from the spirit, therefore the distillation process is much more critical here than it would be elsewhere.

4. Maturation

The new-make spirit that flows from the spirit still is as clear as the water in St Columb's Rill, and legally it can't be called 'whiskey' until it has been matured in an oak barrel for at least three years. However a whiskey might well mature for a decade or two before being ready to bottle. Think of the barrels as lungs, and the maturation process as deep, deep breathing.

When you first fill a cask, about 3% of the liquid will instantly soak into the wooden barrel. Over the years, as the seasons wax and wane, the temperature and humidity will rise and fall, so the porous wooden cask literally breathes in and out.

When the barrel breathes in, the whiskey that had soaked into the wood is forced back into the cask, bringing with it some of the colour and flavour it has leached from the wood. If it is an ex-Bourbon barrel, the colour will be light and the flavour will be vanilla-like; if it's an old sherry butt, the colour will be much darker and the spirit will taste sweetish.

As the casks breathe out, some of the spirit will get pushed right out of the porous wood and will evaporate. A cask will lose around 2% of its volume every year. Walk into any warehouse and you will smell it everywhere – it is called 'The Angels' Share'. There are some very happy angels hanging over Bushmills.

Over ten years, a cask will do a lot of breathing, and that is why a good barrel is important. The wood will contribute subtly to the flavour of the final product, and in the decade or more from harvesting the grain, through mashing, to distilling, to maturation, to pouring yourself a glass, a whiskey will only prove as good as the weakest link in that chain.

The maturation process is important as it imparts to the whiskey the colour and flavour extracted from the wood. Irish whiskey is never matured in new oak barrels, as the raw timber would easily overpower the delicate spirit. However American whiskey has to be matured in new wood; this means there is a constant market for used casks.

Each cask will get used three times at Old Bushmills. Wander through the warehouses and you will see pallets labelled B1, B2, B3 meaning first, second and third fill bourbon, but remember these casks have already been used to mature American whiskey for at least a year. According to Colum Egan, every barrel has a set life span.

"Each time you use a cask, the wood will make a smaller contribution to the whiskey, it kind of gets worn out. After the third use, I feel it's time to send them to the garden centre. You get some beautiful flower displays in our old barrels!"

Bourbon barrels are hugely important at Old Bushmills, but there are many other types of cask here. In fact there seems to have been a long tradition of experimenting with different ageing techniques. Harry Elliott, who worked in maturation for 43 years, remembers using rum, sherry and other exotic woods decades ago. Today's public car park used to be the barrel store.

Nowadays the casks arrive by container ready assembled. The cooper's job then is to check each and every cask. Sometimes a stave may need replacing, or the hoops may need tightening, and there is no point trying to do repairs when a barrel is full of whiskey.

It is possible to buy cheaper barrels on the open market, but with wood, you get what you pay for. The policy here is to do business with one firm that can be trusted. So instead of getting casks from just one distillery, the American oak barrels that will be used by Old Bushmills come from Kelvin Cooperage in Kentucky. They know the kind of quality that

Left: Colum Egan in one of Bushmills' 10 maturation warehouses.

168 | BUSHMILLS

Left and Above: Master Blender Helen Mulholland at work

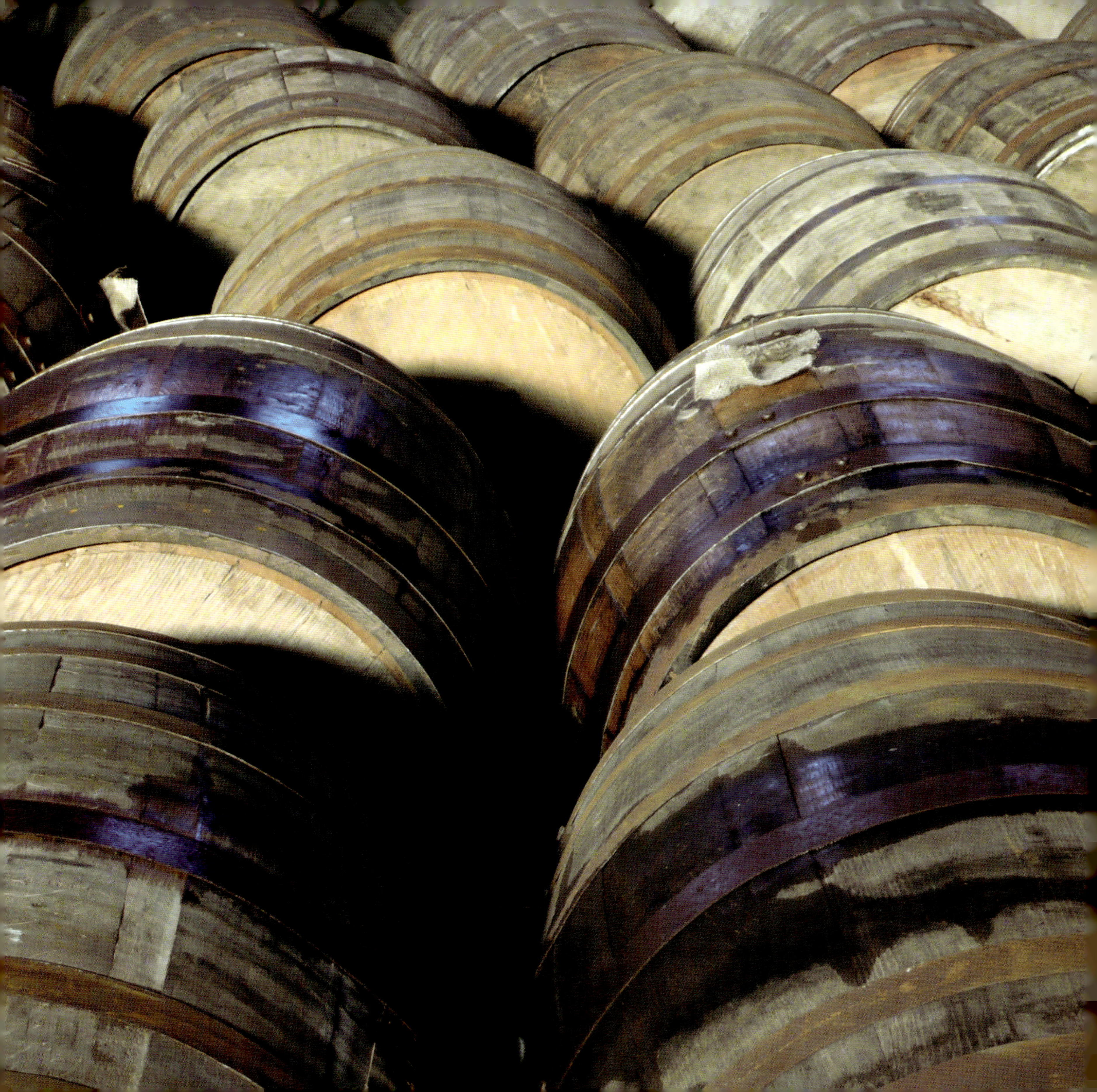

is required and will scan all the American distilleries to find what is needed, so the 200 litre casks used here do not come from Diageo central procurement. Darryl McNally, the Distillery Operations Manager, is proud of their wood policy and their decision to be 'pernickety' and work with Kelvin.

"It's a relationship built on trust. Yes, it's kind of touchy-feely, but it makes for good business, and that makes for good whiskey."

In the warehouses, you will find Irish whiskey maturing in casks that once held Maker's Mark, Ancient Age and Four Roses.

Sherry wood also plays a part in the Old Bushmills story, and its effect can be seen and tasted most noticeably in Black Bush. The sherry butts are made from European oak, cost nearly 15 times as much as bourbon barrels and they can hold twice as much whiskey. All the butts used at Old Bushmills come from just the one source, as you have to be very careful with these casks.

"You can easily over-sherry a whiskey," as Colum Egan puts it. "You have to trust the casks are from a source you know, or you are simply wasting the cost of the cask and 500 litres of whiskey."

It is an expensive mistake to make, so Colum only trusts Antonio Paez who runs a family-owned bodega in Jerez, southern Spain. He fills the casks to be used with Oloroso and then stores them for two years, before they are shipped to Northern Ireland.

Similarly, Sandeman season butts with Tawny Port for two years in Porto, Portugal while Madeira, a small Portuguese island in the Atlantic, is the source of the wood used to finish the Twenty-One-Year-Old.

How do you know when a whiskey is ready? That is the great imponderable. There is always a variation in casks. Even two filled side by side with the same new-make spirit may come out tasting very different. So the rule is: it is ready when it is ready. Therefore it is something the Master Distiller and Master Blender simply keep an eye and a nose on, and they rely on gut instinct and good taste to know when a cask is ready.

5. Blending

Helen Mulholland is the Old Bushmills Master Blender, the first woman in Irish history to hold such an important role.

The various casks of colours, flavours, accents and scents are lined up by Colum. These are what she works with to produce blends like Bushmills Original and Black Bush.

"It's down to how it smells, tastes and how the flavours all work together. We only produce malt whiskey on site – one product. The base spirit has to be perfect. But the maturation in wooden casks is what gives each whiskey its individual character."

With whiskeys varying from cask to cask, and with a brand needing to remain consistent, Helen Mulholland has her hands full. Each blend, and indeed the ten-year-old Single Malt, has its own component vat. The elements that make up, say, a Black Bush are married in a huge 90,000 litre tank, but only 40,000 litres or so are ever drawn off. That leaves 50,000 litres of old whiskey, always there to mix with the new stuff. It helps Helen iron out any remaining 'wrinkles' in a brand. The component vats then are kept topped up at all times.

Finally, visitors to Bushmills who take the tour may notice that the warehouses are numbered curiously. They go from 7 to 17. It is not that the first six have gone missing, it has to do with the age of the place. The distillery is so old that the place was numbered using a system employed by the Customs and Excise when they were resident there.

Left: Casks just filled with new-make Bushmills spirit. It will take at least 3 years of ageing to get whiskey.

ORIGINAL
*A chacun son histoire
BUSHMILLS
IRISH WHISKEY
L'ABUS D'ALCOOL EST DANGEREUX POUR LA SANTÉ. A CONSOMMER AVEC MODÉRATION.

At that time every part of the whiskey making process was numbered, so that the first six 'warehouses' are in fact inside the distillery, and related to the mashing, fermenting and distilling areas. Now you know!

6. Tasting

The final part of the whiskey making process is the enjoyment of the spirit, so it is important to remember what whiskey is and is not about.

For a start whiskey is not about spending lots of money. While you would spend a fortune to enjoy the finest wines in the world, the finest whiskeys are far less taxing on the wallet, and far more accessible. Whiskey then is about honesty, about taking time to relax. It is traditionally a country drink, made by honest people to share and enjoy at the end of a hard day. So why change what has worked for so long, and why make hard work of something that is not?

According to Colum Egan, the best time and place to sip a Bushmills is at dawn on the Giant's Causeway. But let's face it: that is not really that practical. So instead here is my quick guide to Whiskey and the Art of Sensual Pleasure.

Hearing: Break the seal and listen to the *glug, glug, glug* as you put a couple of fingers' worth into a glass.

Sight: Look at the colour, which can tell you a lot about the whiskey in your glass.

Smell: Take a long slow sniff… maybe add a drop of water to open the bouquet.

Touch: Take a good mouthful…

Taste: Even before you swallow you will start tasting the fruits of Old Bushmills.

You will not find 'tasting notes' here. I don't want to tell you what I think – I want you to think for yourself. But if you want to record your own notes (and I sincerely hope you do) please use what follows as a roadmap to help you on your way. And keep it simple:

"As far as tasting notes go," says Colum Egan, "I like to sum up the whiskies with a couple of words…it helps define them, it helps create character."

Left: "We make whiskey for people to enjoy," says Colum Egan, Master Distiller.

Enjoy Irish at its Best responsibly.
You don't get to be
the best because you're the OLDEST.
You get to be the oldest
because you're the BEST.
1608. Original Grant
to Distil.
IRiSH at its BEST
BUSHMILLS
1608
BUSHMILLS
WHISKEY

Left and Above: Bushmills' 'Irish at its Best' advertising campaign

FOUR HUNDRED YEARS IN THE MAKING | 175

176 | BUSHMILLS

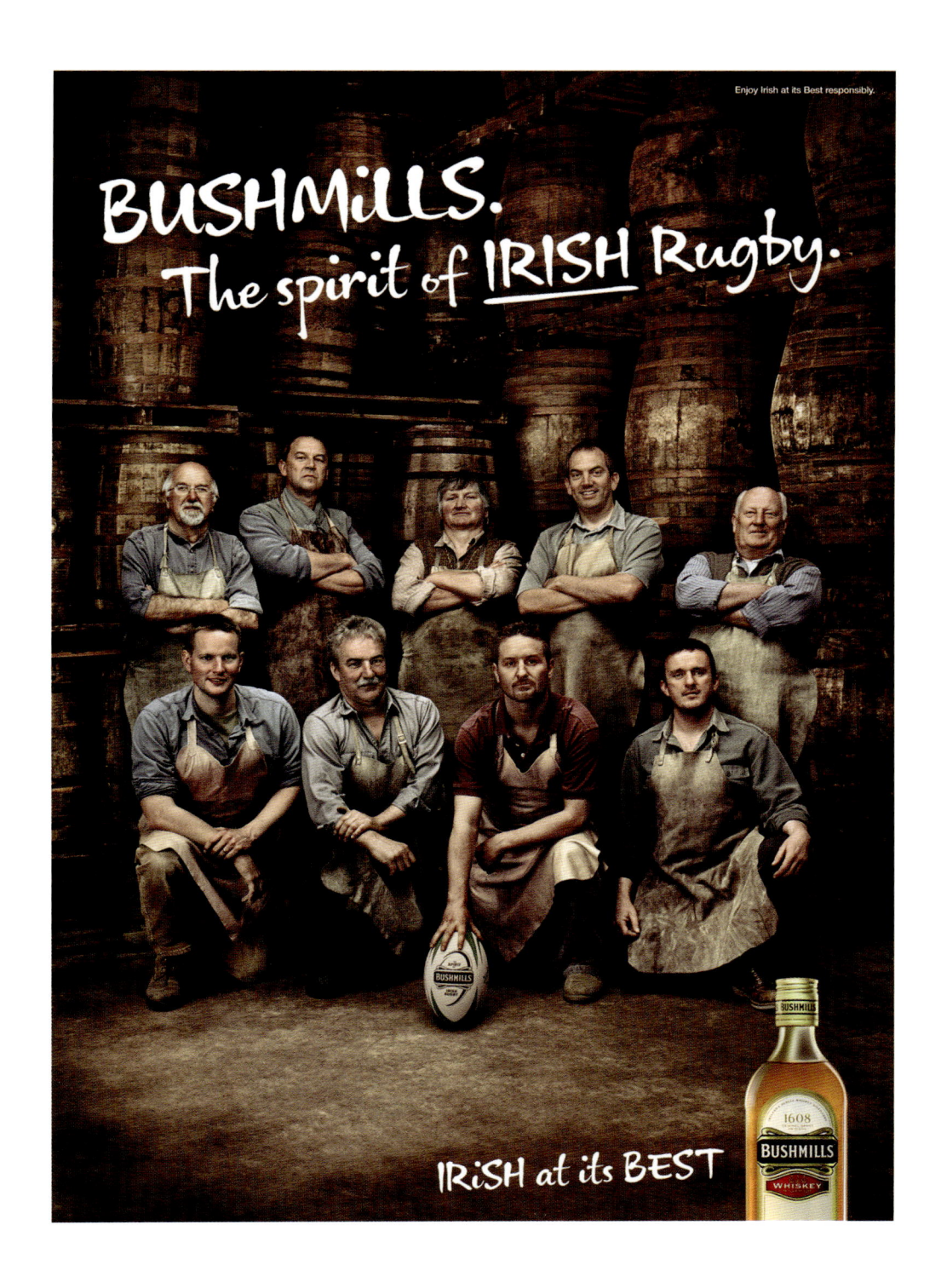

Left and Above: Bushmills' "Irish at its Best" advertising campaign

Bushmills Original

Key Words: Fruity Vanilla

It is very unusual in the world of whiskey to have blends and malts selling under the same name. But this is Old Bushmills, and here things have always been a bit quirky and a bit different.

This gentle giant has been around in one form or another since grain whiskey was first produced at Coleraine in 1954, though you could trace its heritage back even further, to when the Boyds blended Bushmills malt with grain whiskeys sourced from elsewhere in Ireland. It is not surprising that over time this brand has been called lots of things, including Home Trade, Three Star and White Bush, but nowadays Bushmills Original seems to do the trick.

Although in the United States this whiskey outsells all the other Bushmills whiskey combined, on the home market it was rather neglected by its previous owners.

Guide to Tasting:
The whiskey has a nice light colour. Colour can tell you a lot. There is no reddish tint here, so you won't taste any sherry wood. This is a typically bourbon-matured whiskey.

It is a friendly whiskey, with a welcoming nose that almost pulls you into the glass. The nose can smell things in parts per billion, so breathe in the whiskey and see what sparks into your mind. But don't stay too long, or the alcohol will anaesthetise your nasal passages and you will smell nothing.

Add some water. This doesn't water it down – not unless you add a huge splash, that is. So add a couple of drops and watch it eddy in the whiskey. Whiskey is kind of oily, so what you are doing here is breaking the surface, giving the aromas a chance to move about and release their flavour.

Expect peach, hints of the still house here. The vanilla, which comes from the American oak casks, is gentle. Leave it in the glass for a while, however, and it gets stronger and more pronounced.

This is an easy whiskey, made to enjoy. At around five years old, it is not a complicated whiskey, but it does not have to be. There is a lot to appreciate here if you take your time and if you are new to whiskey, this is a great place to start.

Finally it is great value, and a yardstick to measure all other whiskeys against.

Black Bush

Key Words: Nutty Sweetness

Black Bush is the second famous blend to come from the North Antrim distillery. It is the lovable rogue of the bunch, so not surprisingly it has a hugely loyal following right around the globe, and some very famous fans.

The whiskey is a high malt blend, but it is the grain that is really interesting. You see unlike regular grain whiskey, which is made in a continuous still, this is made in a traditional copper still. A small amount of it goes into Bushmills Original, but in Black Bush it really comes into its own. It has a fantastic texture and great mouth feel, particularly as a large proportion of the whiskey is matured in sherry wood.

Hold the whiskey up to the light and you will catch the amber glow. This burnished copper heart is particular to Black Bush and quite unlike anything else.

Guide to Tasting:
The nose here is fuller, bigger, bolder and brighter than Bushmills Original.

Add some water and release an even more intense blast of aroma. You may get a warm hint of a Spanish bodega – that is the sherry wood at work – but notice how it is not overpowering. Here the spirit and the wood are in perfect harmony, one singing to the other on the tip of your nose.

When you sip, you will get the unique mouth feel that comes from the grain whiskey. It somehow does not feel wet. Black Bush just glides around the mouth like liquid silk.

The *finish* is what we call the flavours that are left kicking around your mouth after you swallow. Sometimes a whiskey's finish is short, sometimes it goes on and on, and on occasion it can be rather nasty. Here however the quality of the casks is reflected in the sweet warm glow that toasts the back of the throat.

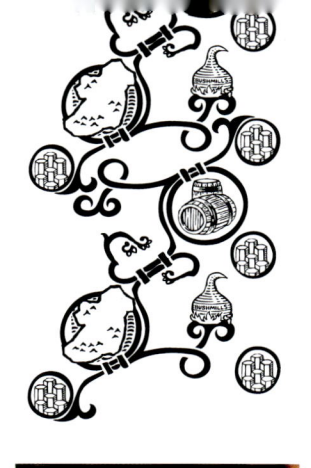

FOUR HUNDRED YEARS IN THE MAKING

Bushmills 1608

Key Words: Spicy Malt

Every anniversary deserves to be celebrated. Not many of us get to party on our 400th birthday, so it was clear a very special whiskey was needed for a very special occasion. But where to start?

Every Master Distiller experiments. They play around with grain, with mashing and distilling, but mostly maturation as it is the easiest. Not all the experiments work, but some do, and this is how change happens.

"We always do different things," Colum explained. "But we're not trying to show how clever we are, we are simply [being] innovative; trying to find new ways of making great whiskey."

So at any moment in time there are a range of different whiskeys maturing in the warehouses, but not all of them work and not all are ready.

When Colum Egan went rummaging in the Old Bushmills warehouses, he found lots of interesting casks laid down by his predecessors, but he was intrigued by one particular batch. Some years previously the Master Distiller had made whiskey using crystal malt. Although common enough in breweries, especially in micro-breweries, where it is used to give beer extra mouthfeel, no other distillery Colum had ever heard of had used crystal malt to make whiskey.

Excited as Colum was, "it just wasn't totally there". So he added just a few per cent of old grain whiskey. "And that added the balance I was looking for," he said. "The grain pulls it together."

Ronnie Brennan remembers doing the mash for the crystal malt run.

"The distillery does a lot of unusual stuff, but most of it never sees the light of day. But I remember well doing 25 mashes of crystal malt, because there was a very different smell from it: and not a nice one either! It was very strong and to be honest I didn't think it would amount to much."

However Ronnie now agrees that his mash of crystal malt has made an exceptional whiskey. This just goes to show that there is an art to distilling as well as a science.

Colum Egan is clearly rather proud of Bushmills 1608.

"Everyone was expecting us to release a new Single Malt for the anniversary, so going with a blend was, I feel, brave and innovative. But we didn't do it to be pig-headed, we just went with the best whiskey we could find at that time, and it just happened to be a blend."

Crystal malt is made by preheating the drum that will be used to malt the barley. The barley then hits a hot drum and is toasted before being blasted with air at 500°C. This literally crystallises the simple sugars that coat the grain. If you bite a grain of crystal malt, it has a crisp golden shell that cracks like a sugar coated sweet. The flavour is similar to the crisp topping on crème brûlée.

This results in a whiskey that is similar to the ten-year-old malt, but strangely different. For the record, this is a new release, not to be confused with an earlier, now discontinued whiskey which was called '1608 Reserve', and sported a purple and blue label.

Guide to Tasting:

Bushmills 1608 is a premium blended Irish whiskey. At the heart of 1608 is that crystal malt whiskey, and it does indeed

10 Year Old Single Malt

Key Words: Malty Chocolate

give a unique sensual mouthfeel. The malt is matured in a combination of American oak casks and Spanish Oloroso Sherry butts, which lends extra layers of complexity to an already fine dram.

More often than not, grain whiskey is firmer than malt. You can normally feel it as you swallow, but here the grain is so soft that it is unnoticeable. It all works so well that picking out the individual notes would be like trying to pick apart a fine piece of music. Don't bother, instead just let it wash over you.

Bushmills 1608 is bottled at the slightly higher than normal strength of 46% abv for optimum flavour development, so you may need to add a wee drop more water than normal.

There has been a ten-year-old single malt from Old Bushmills on sale since the late nineteenth century. So they must be doing something right.

In the ten-year-old, you can really start to appreciate the Bushmills malt DNA; that is, the signature that runs right through the range. Younger versions of this malt can be found in all the blends, but here for the first time it can be tasted on its own.

"What we do with the Ten-Year-Old," says Colum Egan, "is we mature, or age, a portion of it, just a small amount, in sherry-seasoned casks, just to give it a hint of that sweetness."

Indeed there is not a huge amount of sherry influence here, either in the colour or in the taste. This is a very clean, malty whiskey – indeed if you want to know what whiskey writers mean by *malty*, smell this whiskey.

Guide to Tasting:
Colum calls the ten-year-old "a very easy, everyday sipping malt". And indeed if you hold a glass of this malt on its side and then drizzle in some water, you will see it eddy and spin – catch the hints of malt and chocolate as they spiral out of the glass.

This is a very charming whiskey, one even non-whiskey drinkers warm to. It is light, so expect to find honey on the edge of your cheeks. Some people get hints of pastry, some of apples: I get a far off rumble of fine liquorice, but many do not. That is the point. We are all individuals and we all have our own opinions, so don't take my word for it.

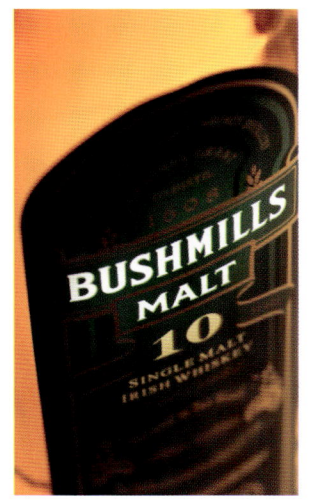

FOUR HUNDRED YEARS IN THE MAKING | 181

16 Year Old Single Malt

Key Words: Honeyed Almond

Explore: there is so much to be enjoyed here right to the very end, when you might feel a slightly dry, fruity brush on the back of the throat – *interesting*. I don't know where it comes from and you shouldn't care: it just feels nice.

The age statement here simply means that the youngest whiskey used is at least sixteen years old. In any old whiskey you will find the influence of the wood more apparent, but here maturation is taken to a new level with whiskey matured in not one, but three different types of cask.

This single malt was launched in 1996 after Irish Distillers bought 100 port pipes from Sandeman. Fifty of the casks were sent to Midleton, but a Jameson port finish never materialised. However they had more success in Co. Antrim, where Bushmills malt matured in bourbon, sherry and port wood proved a winner.

This brand is pretty much a half-and-half mix of sixteen-year-old bourbon and sixteen-year-old sherry-matured whiskey that are married for 9 months in a port cask. But this is high-wire stuff. Old whiskey is fragile and can easily be overwhelmed by the wood, so after 4 months in the port pipe, the malt is nosed and tasted, and thereafter a very close eye is kept on it.

"It's ready when it's ready, as every port cask is different," said Colum Egan. "Like sherry, port can be very overpowering, so the maturation can't go on too long. We don't take our eyes off it! But I tell you when it comes to emptying the casks, the boys love tipping that stuff. There's a great smell!"

In a whiskey of this age, evaporation is also a problem. Remember that every year a whiskey matures, it loses 2% of its volume, so after sixteen years that's nearly 28% of a loss. Nearly a third of the barrel has simply disappeared.

21 Year Old Single Malt

Key Words: Dark Chocolate Raisins

Guide to Tasting:
The contribution that maturation makes to a great whiskey can really be appreciated here. Expect to find a fruity spiciness, also the chocolate that was in the ten-year-old is still here, but it is darker and search for marzipan or praline chocolate. At the end comes the unmistakable port wine finish.

If the sixteen-year-old is a 'high-wire act', then this rather remarkable old whiskey is 'a barrel over Niagara Falls' stuff. Launched in 2001, this malt is a 50:50 combination of whiskey matured for 19 years in a combination of bourbon and sherry casks, which is then finished in Madeira drums for another 2 years.

But whiskey matures far more quickly in Ireland that in Scotland, so 21 years is a long, long time. Older doesn't always equal better, so choosing the right wood is crucial. Over time bad sherry casks can add an unpleasant note of sulphur: leave a floral malt in bourbon wood for too long and all you will taste are splinters.

At the end of 19 years the whiskeys are vatted, and refilled into casks that once contained Madeira. However to get the contribution of the Madeira just right, the finishing process can take up to another two years.

Only 900 cases of this whiskey are produced annually. Most of the stock goes to the USA, the biggest market. There is no magic tap in the wall – every drop has to have been laid down at least 21 years ago. This means that there are no extra stocks of this whiskey to be had until 2010. This is a malt to be enjoyed on any rare occasion you can think of.

Guide to Tasting:
The twenty-one-year-old has a deeper, darker, stronger character than anything else produced by the distillery. The chocolate is very dark now, but almost with a clean minty edge. The toffee is darker and the raisins are very chewy. It is a very careful balancing act between spirit, wood and time:

FOUR HUNDRED YEARS IN THE MAKING | 183

get any one of them wrong and this will not work. Of the three, time is the most mercurial and that is something not even Einstein worked out.

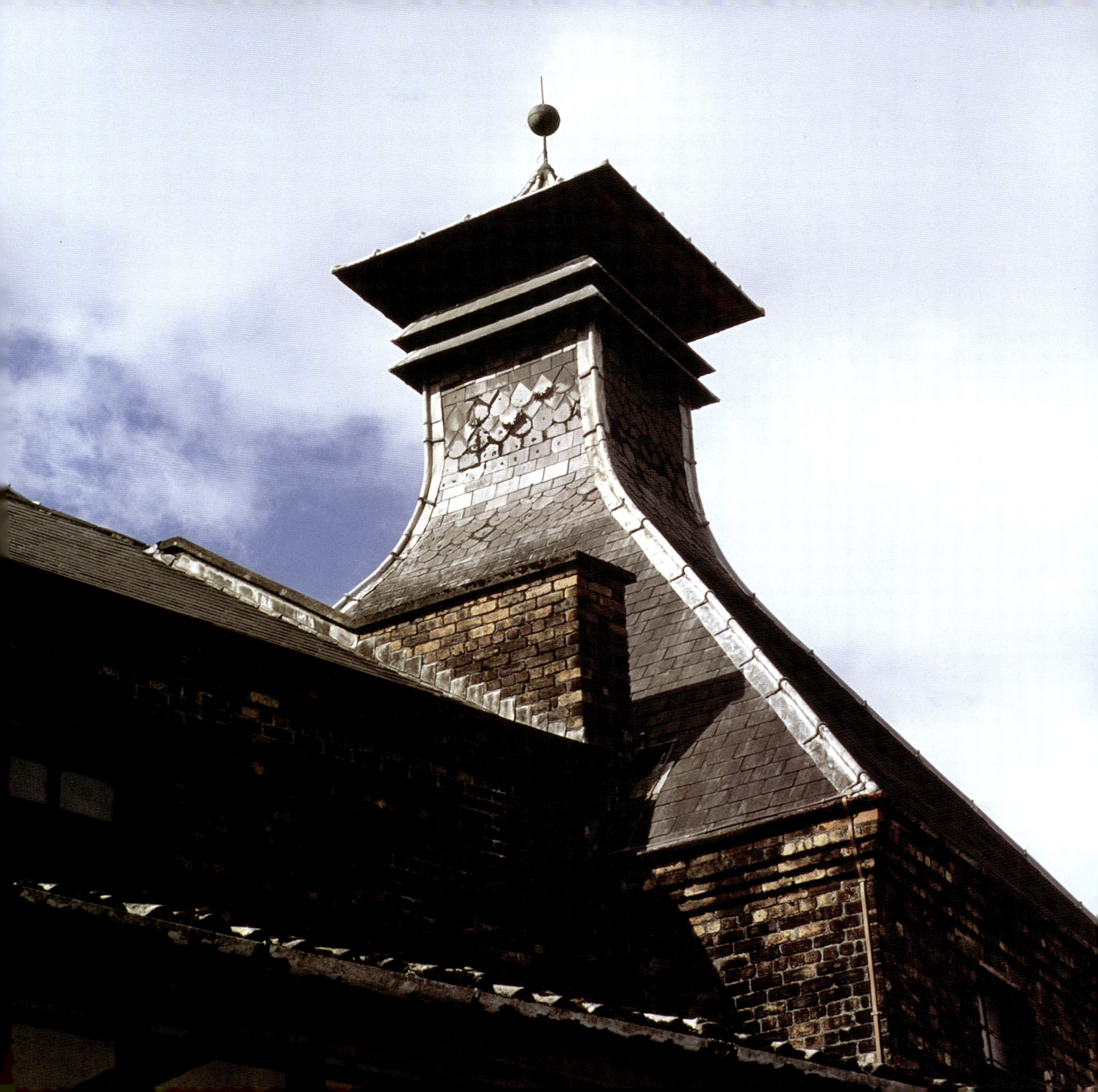

Acknowledgements

The publisher wishes to thank the following organisations and people who gave permission to reproduce work in copyright.

pp. 1, 2 and front cover Trade edition, 6, 7, 8, 10, 12-13, 40, 41, 42, 45, 54-55, 56-57, 58-59, 60-61, 62-63, 74, 76-77, 78-79, 80-81, 82, 84-85, 86-87, 88, 90-91, 104, 106-107, 116, 124, 125, 126, 128-129, 130, 131, 132, 133, 134, 137, 138-139, 144, 148, 152, 153, 154, 156-157, 160, 163, 166, 168, 170, 172, 174, 175, 176, 177, 178, 179, 180, 181, 182, 183, 185, 190-191 and front of Corporate edition dustjacket, 192 and PB front cover © The Old Bushmills Distillery Co. Ltd

pp. 52, 102 and HB back cover, 113, 114-115 and PB back cover, 118-119, 120, 122-123, 140: Historical Photographs, Lynne Bryce and the staff at the Old Bushmills Distillery

pp. 32, 34, 39, 64-65: Other historical pictures and illustrations: Christine McCafferty, Diageo Archive

pp. 98-99 © *Belfast Telegraph*

p. 169 © *Belfast Telegraph* / Ian Trevithick

pp. 14, 20 © istockphoto.com/Duncan Walker

p. 66 © istockphoto.com/Linda Steward

p. 96 © istockphoto.com/Chris Scredon

pp. 136, 142-143, 145, 146-147, 150-151, 158, 162, 164 © Peter Mulryan

The publisher would also like to thank the Linenhall Library and in particular Kristian J. L. McComb for their help in sourcing the following images:

pp. 44, 92 (*The Album of the Giant's Causeway*)
p. 47 (*Thom's Directory*, 1861)
p. 68-69 Dunville distillery
p. 94 (*Coleraine and District*)

Additional images sourced from the Library of Congress:

pp. 38-39 (Paris Exhibition, 1889), 50 (wood engraving, *Harper's Weekly*, 1879), 70 (bootleggers apprehended by Police, 1921), 72-73 (Prohibition raid, 1921), 108 (Empire State Building)

Index

1608   11, 19, 22, 23, 139
1608 Club   141, 142, *150-151*
1608 Reserve   180

advertising   *40*, *41*, *47*, 77, *90*, 91, 93, *94*, *104*, *106*, *107*,
               109, 112, *116*, *124*, *125*, *130*, *131*, *132*,
               133, 137, *174*, *175*, *176*, *177*
alcohol   17, 19, 27, 31, 33, 35, 55, 57, 71, 157, 165, 178
alembic   17
al-kuhl   17
Ambassador De Luxe Scotch   105
Anderson, Molly (1608 club)   147, *150-151*
Angels' Share   167
aqua vitae   15, 16, 18, 19, 22, 24
aquavite   23
Austin Nichols   127
Avoniel distillery   33, 69, 87
awards   37, *39*, *40-41*, 43

barley   45, 47, 67, 83, 95, *96*, 97, 99, 100,
               112, 141, 155, *158*, 159, 180
Barnard, Alfred   25, 43, 45, 53, 93
Bass-Charrington   115
Belfast   27, 30, 33, 36, 37, 46, 48, 49, 55, 67, 69,
               75, 81, 83, 87, 89, 97, 99, 100, 103, 111
Black Bush   *8*, 75, 77, 95, 112, 159, 171, **179**
Black Death, the   7
Black, John (1608 club)   *150-151*
Black, Thomas   93
Blitz   48, 97, *98-99*, 99
Boyd, Austin   83, 109, 112, 121
Boyd, James Steen   46, 49, 51

Boyd, Samuel Wilson   73, 75, 79, 81, 83
Boyd, Wilson   83, 85, 87, 89, 100, 103, 105, 112
Brennan, Ronnie (1608 club)   142, *150-151*, 159, 161, 180
Bronfman, Sam   119, 121
Bushmills   9, 11, 15, 18, 23, 25, 26, 27, 29, 30, 37, 45, 46,
               47, 51, 55, 81, 83, 87, 95, 99, 100, *102*, 103, 105, 112, 119,
               121, *122*, *126*, 127, *128*, 129, 135, 137, 141, 142, 147, 155,
               159, 165, 167, 171, 173, 178, 181, 182, *190-191*, *192*
   whiskeys   8, 9, 39
Bushmills 1608   *152*, **180**
Bushmills Original   *152*, 159, 171, **178**, 179, 180, 181

Cantrell & Cochrane (C&C)   127
cask   81, 91, 98, 145, 157, 165, 169, *170*
                      176, 177, 178, 179, 180, 181
cat (Bushmills distillery)   163
Chambers, Billy (1608 club)   139, *150-151*
Charrington   109, **111**, 113, 114, 117, 119
Chichester, Sir Arthur   23
Coffey, Aeneas   8, 10, 11
Coffey Still   31, *32*, 33
Coleraine   4, 5, 6, 7, 8, 14, 19, 24, 26, 28, 29,
                      33, 36, 39, 42, 43
Coleraine (County of)   21, 22, 24
Coleraine distillery   55, 81, 89, *92*, **93**, *94*, 95, 103, 112,
                       121, 142, 147, 159, 178
Coleraine Chronicle   43
Comber distillery (Upper Comber/Old Comber)   81, 87, 100
cooper   30, *52*, *74*, *114-115*, 142, *149*, 167
Cork Distilleries Company   117
Cork Distilling Company   117
Customs and Excise   101, 171
   see also Excise
'Cutty Sark'   73

FOUR HUNDRED YEARS IN THE MAKING | 187

Depression, the	81
Diageo	135, 171
distillation	22, 27, 31, 55, 85, 95, 115, 165, 167
Distillers Company Limited	36
draff	161, 165
Dunville distillery	33, *68-69*, 81, 100
Egan, Colum *see Master Distiller*	
Elizabeth I, queen of England	18, 19, *20*, 21
Elliott, Harry (1608 Club)	*145*, *146-147*, 147, *150-151*, 167
Excise	25, 26, 27, 28, 30, 31, 98, 169
fermentation	*57*, 165
Garvin, Kenny	*137*, 165
GC&C	127
Giant's Causeway	11, 29, 45
Gilbey's	109, 127
Glen distillery (Cork)	45
Great Universal Stores (GUS)	103, 111, 112
grist	161
Guinness	95, 97, 99, 100, 126, 135
Henry II, king of England	*14*, 15
'Irish at its best'	115, 137, *175*, *176*, *177*
Irish Distillers	95, **117**, 119, 121, 123, 127, 129, 135, 159, 182
Irish Sea	17, 19, 67
Irish Whiskey and Distillers Association	107
J&B	105
James I, king of England	21
Jameson	30, 69, 73, 81, 109, 117, 127, 129, 135, 137, 182
Johnnie Walker	105, 112

Jubilee Malt	49
Kaplan, Col. Henry	103
Kilbeggan distillery	81, 109
Killowen distillery	95, 99, 100, 142, 147
Laudabiliter	15
lemonade	149
Le Savage, Sir William	15
licence	18, 19, 23, 24, 26, 89, 97, 100
licence to distil	23, 139, 141
patent to distil	19
malt whiskey	39, 45, 49, 91, 93, 169, 178
maltose	161
mash tun	*80*, 83, 139, 142, *160*, 161, *162*, *163*, 171
Master Blender	*152*, *168*, *169*, 171
Master Distiller	134, *137*, 149, *152*, *160*, 161, *166*, 171, 180
McCook, Watson	142, *149*, *153*
McCool, Finn	11
McKibben, James	29, 30, 37
McMullen, Belina (1608 club)	147, *150-151*
MacNaghten, Sir Francis Workman	29
Midleton distillery (Old Midleton)	30, 81, 119, 121, 159, 182
Morrison, James Watt	83, 85, 87, 95, 97, 100
Mulholland, Helen *see Master Blender*	
Murphy's distillery (Cork)	30
New York	49, 51, 73, 89, 105, *108*, **109**
New York Times, The	71, 89, 109
Nugent, Chester	97, 100
Nugent, Granville	97
Nugent, James	97
O'Donnell, Hugh	19

188 | BUSHMILLS

O'Neill, Hugh	19, 21, 22	sherry butt	*84-85*, *114*, 167, 171, 181
Old Bushmills distillery	11, 18, 23, 37, 46, 75, 95, 83, 121	silent spirit	31, 33, 35, 46, 55, 57
Old Bushmills Liqueur Whiskey	77	Single Malt	45, **46**, 47, 73, 87, 93, 127, 149, 159, 171, 180, 181, 182, 183
Old Bushmills Pure Malt Whiskey	45		
Old Glyn Bush	47, 48	Single Malt, 10-year-old	*154*, **181**
Ordnance Survey Memoirs	29	Single Malt, 16-year-old	**182**
		Single Malt, 21-year-old	**183**
Paris Exhibition 1889	*38-39*, 39, *40*, *41*, 147	Spanish Armada	19
Partition	**67**	SS *Bushmills*	49, 51
Patent Still	32, 33, *35*, 57, 77	St Columb's Rill	11, 45, *60*, 157, 167
Pernod Ricard	127, 129, 135	Statutes of Kilkenny	18
Philip, king of Spain	21		
Phillips, Sir Thomas	22, 23, 24, 27	Taylor, Robert	93
Plantation of Ulster	4, 5, 6, 21, 22	Thompson, Uel	*142-143*
poitín	26, 27, 29, 37	Tullamore distillery	51, 81
poteen	**27**, 29	Tullamore Dew	109, 127, 129
Pope Adrian IV	15		
Pope Gregory XIII	21	*uisce beatha*	12, 17, 18
pot-still whiskey	31, 33, *34*, 44, 67	usquebaugh	18
Powers	30, 69, 73, 81, 109, 117, 129		
Prohibition	27, *70*, 71, *72-73*, 73, 75, 89, 95, 119	Victoria, queen of England	47, 149
see also Volstead Act		Volstead Act	71, 89
River Bush	11, 12, *13*, 25, 45, *58-59*, 157	wash back	*56*, *82*, 83, *162*, 165
Roe's distillery	30	Watt's distillery	33
Royal Commission	35, 57	whiskey	8, 9, 11, 16, 18, 19, 22, 24, 27, 28, 30, 31, 33, 35, 36, 37, 39, 43, 45, 47, 48, 49, 51, 53, 55,57, 59, 67, 71, 73, 75, 77, 81, 83, 87, 89, 93, 95,97, 99, 100, 101, 105, 109, 111, 112, 115, 117, 119, 121, **127**, 129, 135, 137, 139, 141, 142, 147, 149, 155, 157 **161**
Royal Irish distillery	69, 81		
rummagers	*88*, 165		
Savage, Sir Robert	15		
Savages of the Ards, The	15	whisky	31, 33, **35**, 36, 43, 53, 67, 73, 165
Scotch blends	36	Wolfson, Sir Isaac	103, 105, 111
Seagram	119, 121, 123, 127, 129, 135	World War, First	101
Shah of Persia	39, *40*, *41*	World War, Second	95, 97, 100, 101, 105, 111, 119
sherry	167, 171, 178, 179, 182, 183	wort	161, 165